How to win a
final-year student

D0358266

378.17 RAC

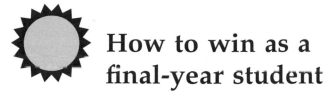

How to win as a final-year student

Essays, exams and employment

Phil Race

Open University Press
Buckingham · Philadelphia

Open University Press
Celtic Court
22 Ballmoor
Buckingham
MK18 1XW

email: enquiries@openup.co.uk
world wide web: www.openup.co.uk

and

325 Chestnut Street
Philadelphia, PA 19106, USA

First Published 2000

A catalogue record of this book is available from the British Library

ISBN   0 335 20511 9 (pb)   0 335 20512 7 (hb)

Library of Congress Cataloging-in-Publication Data
Race, Philip.
      How to win as a final-year student : essays, exams, and employment /
Phil Race.
          p. cm.
      Includes bibliographical references and index.
      ISBN 0-335-20512-7 (hb) – ISBN 0-335-20511-9 (pb)
      1. Universities and colleges – Handbooks, manuals, etc.   2. College
seniors – Handbooks, manuals, etc.   3. Study skills – Handbooks, manuals,
etc.   4. College graduates – Employment – Handbooks, manuals, etc. I. Title.
LB2324.R33 2000
378.1'98–dc21

                                                                                                99-050030

Typeset by Graphicraft Limited, Hong Kong
Printed in Great Britain by Biddles Ltd, Guildford and King's Lynn

Contents

 # Acknowledgements

I would like to express my appreciation for the help and support provided by Open University Press in the journey between this book being just an idea, and what you see before you now. Shona Mullen is responsible for the idea that a book could be needed for final-year students in the first place, and for continued encouragement and advice all the way through its creation. The comments from the three anonymous referees were extremely valuable, and continue to add much to the value of the completed book. I would also like to thank Jon Ingoldby, the copy editor, who not only caused extensive improvements to the wording and layout of the book, but also read the content very diligently and came up with a number of valuable suggestions for clarifications, additions and useful deletions!

Finally, thanks to many students and lecturers, in my workshops on study skills, teaching and assessment. Their comments, views – and problems – have provided my inspiration for this book, and I hope the overall result will lead to a better final year for many students.

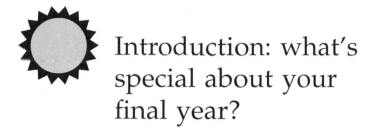

Introduction: what's special about your final year?

▶ **It only happens once, so you may as well do it well**

Many successful graduates look back, years later, at their final year at university as a time when they pulled out all the stops. However, most also look back and wish they'd done it somewhat differently. Some remember throwing everything they had at the challenges of that year, but wish they'd done more to get the balance right. Even more look back and wish they'd put more energy into tackling the whole of that final year. You can learn from their experience, their mistakes, and the challenges they faced. You've still got time to strike a better balance than most.

The world of higher education is your scene for the campaign to come. It's a somewhat strange world. Everyone around you seems to know what they're doing, and yet many of the people you know outside this world don't understand it. Most people in the population at large have not experienced it. Some have tried it, and it didn't work for them. Those who have succeeded may have forgotten how they achieved that success.

Many successful graduates look back at their final year with a significant list of 'if only . . .' provisos in their minds. 'If only I'd known how much it was going to count for, and that it was only one year in my life, I'd have done things quite differently' they often say. You're in a position to eliminate such future 'if onlys'. You already know it's an important year. You can decide to give it your best shot. That doesn't mean working unbelievably hard, but it does mean working smart. That's what this book is about.

What's the difference between now and earlier years?

To be reading this book, you've already survived at least one year at university, and maybe two or more years. You know what it's like in these earlier years. The chances are that you've already done a great deal of growing in your time in higher education. You're probably quite a different person from the first-time undergraduate you were, only a short while ago. Much of this growing will be as an independent person, and some of it will have been as an autonomous learner. Alternatively, you may be a part-time student, and have done most of your growing in the world outside universities. In either case, the biggest difference about your final year is that it counts more. If you win your campaign, you'll get a piece of paper which will serve you well throughout the rest of your life. If you lose your campaign, you won't!

▶ **What's *your* final year for?**

This book aims to help you with *how* to tackle your final year. Have you sometimes stopped, perhaps when things were getting you down, and asked yourself 'How did I get myself into doing all this?' Some sensible, and really important, questions to put to yourself, not just when you're feeling stressed, are:

- *Why* am I doing this final year?
- What's in it for me?
- Why is it going to be worth my time and effort?

You may think these are obvious questions to ask, and that you've already sorted out why you're doing your final year. However, it's quite possible that you've arrived at the threshold of your final year without having had the time or opportunity to really think *why* you are where you are. At the start of your first year, you probably had good answers to the question 'why?', but you may not have revisited your rationale for some time. Just in case, before you start using this book to help you to succeed in your final year, I'd like you to remind yourself of your own rationale for being at university. The task which follows has a number of steps, but don't put off doing it – it doesn't take long, and can pay huge dividends in terms of sorting out the rationale which will underpin your final-year strategy.

Task: establishing your rationale – the 'diamond-9'

1 Take a sheet of plain paper.

2 Fold it into thirds both ways, and tear it into nine equal pieces. (Alternatively, take part of a pad of post-its – any size, any colour.)

3 Spend a few minutes distancing yourself from what *others* (such as parents, tutors, lecturers, partner, friends) think are the reasons *why* you're doing your final year now.

4 Think about doing your final year now.

5 Think about *your* dreams, ambitions and hopes.

6 Ask yourself the question 'What do I *want* to be as a result of this final year?'

7 Remind yourself you're not asking yourself 'What am I *expected* to become?'

8 Allow yourself to think of absolutely *anything* that you might want to be, even if it's got nothing whatsoever to do with the degree course you're about to finish.

9 You've got nine chances – get started. On each of your pieces of paper (or Post-its) write down *one* thing you may want to become, or achieve, as a result of succeeding with your final year now. These things can include jobs (tinker, tailor, soldier, spy etc.), and attributes (power, wealth, fame, respect etc.), and all sorts of other 'things' that you may dream of being in a few years' time. Get writing, one 'thing' per piece of paper, till you've used up all nine.

10 If your mind is still whirring, make a few more pieces of paper the same size, and continue, one idea on each.

11 Now put your nine reasons (or top nine, if you did more) for doing your final year (for that's what each of your pieces of paper now amounts to), into a 'diamond-9' layout, with the most important or most significant one at the top, then the next most important one in position two, and so on, till you've made a pattern like a nine of diamonds, as shown on the next page.

Did you notice how hard it is to put your ambitions and dreams into an order of priority? That's why I suggested separate pieces of paper, or better still, Post-its. You can continue to shuffle and rearrange them. Tomorrow, your order of priority may well be different. The next day you may think of yet another important 'thing' or attribute that you want to become or achieve as a direct result of this, your final year.

I suggest that you look at what *changes* in your plans for yourself may have been suggested by this process of thinking what *you* really want from your life and career. The better you know *why* you're doing this final year, the more ready you will be to look at:

- *what* to do;
- *when* to do it; and
- *how* to go about it.

Without the 'why', the rest are just academic. The 'why' agenda needs to belong most definitely to you, not just to other people and their expectations of you, or their hopes about you.

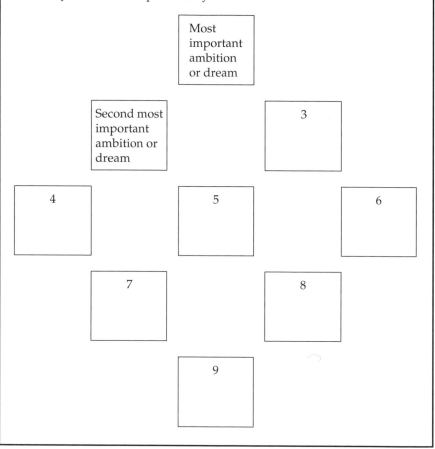

I suggest that you repeat the 'diamond-9' exercise from time to time during your final year. As you get deeper into your subject matter, and as you find out more about job possibilities, don't be surprised that new and more interesting things occur to you. Keep your diamond-9 polished and up to date. Keep it yours. Put it somewhere where you can see it most days – on a wall, for example. If other people ask you what it is, explain it to them. This is good consolidation of *your* ambitions; explaining them to someone else helps you to believe in them yourself. Mapping out life prospects in this way may be an idea they will want to take up for themselves, and you can help them get started. It reminds them, and you, about what makes each other tick, in the context of that final year.

▶ What are the main challenges?

The main challenges can be summed up in a nutshell:

- to get your degree, and do as well as you would like to in that;
- to get your postgraduate career underway;
- to retain your sanity, health, and sense of proportion.

There are all sorts of other things you may achieve during your final year, but most of these could be achieved later, and are not as urgent or as important as the short list above.

You may like to compare your ideas of what the main challenges are with those of some people who tackled their final year successfully, and went on to research or to lecturing appointments. I asked just such a group what they felt the main challenges had been and what would have helped them (or did actually help them) cope successfully with those challenges. The following is based on their replies:

Examples of challenges	Potential or actual avenues of help
• Catching up; coping with stress; trying not to appear too neurotic. • Getting to sleep.	• An informed and non-judgemental listener. • Less drinking etc. in my second year!
• Stress. • Dissertation – problems with a group dissertation context. • Motivation. • Heavy first semester, light second semester.	• Swimming. Took up smoking again! • Continued group meetings sorted this out; spoke to supervisor about the problems. • Talking with others. • Help on time and task management?
• Exams. • Projects.	• Advice on time management and tactics. • More curiosity would have helped.
• Distinguishing between which areas were important and which were trivial.	• Guidance sought as to which subjects were critical, and time management skills.

Examples of challenges	Potential or actual avenues of help
• Ability to manage time. • Producing posters, and seminars. • Survival!	• Would have been helped by a nicer timetable in the first semester, and a slave who could cut and paste for me!
• Difficulty in relaxing, to aid memory skills and avoid mental blanks.	• Kept up with friends, social life, sport, and kept my interest in the subject area.
• Writing dissertation. • Coping with husband's planned career change. • Coping with a teenage daughter and a stroppy 8-year-old son!	• Improve selectivity of studying. • Change husband? • Full time nanny!
• Getting my degree at all.	• I shouldn't have got drunk and wasted so much time in my second year.
• Guilt. • Motivation (lack of). • Prioritizing – difficulty of.	• Learn to work for its own sake. • Choose early the subjects you love. • Tricks from others, e.g. question spotting.
• Tackling the boring bits.	• Knowing when to stop, when there was enough to pass.
• Fitting in fun, socializing. • Stress, anxiety, panic.	• Make better use of summer holidays. • Starting earlier, knowing when to stop, relaxation.
• Reading and understanding. • Self-organization.	• Improved when given feedback on academic work. • Coursework assessment aided revision.
• Having to do courses which I didn't like.	• Concentrating on things I liked, and going into more depth with these.

As you can see, there's a lot of common ground between the problems they experienced and the solutions that worked for them. This book is intended to help you to find your own solutions to such problems.

▶ **What are your strengths?**

To have got as far as the threshold of your final year, you can't be bad at studying. You've already learned a great deal about all sorts of subjects, and forgotten more than you may care to remember! You've already passed exams, and got satisfactory grades for coursework. You know a lot about how assessment works in higher education. There aren't any major surprises lying in wait for you. You've already built up your strategies for getting by in your studies and assessments. You may know of holes in your technique, but you've got all sorts of strengths which can continue to see you through your final year.

How's your confidence?

Confidence is important. Many would say that it's the most important factor predetermining your success. One of the main aims of this book is to help you confront yourself to find out more about how you tick, so that you can develop confidence based upon known good habits, good attitudes and good strategies.

You need at least two kinds of confidence for your final year. One is confidence in your academic ability, to help you to *demonstrate* that ability in your final-year exams and other assessment-related activities that will contribute towards your academic success. The other is confidence in getting a grip on making your next moves, and beginning your post-graduate career. This kind of confidence is reflected by how well you set about applying for jobs, and how well you show at interviews what kind of person you really are, matching what you show to what employers are seeking. These add up to a third kind of confidence, which is more subtle, and harder to earn. This is confidence that you are achieving a sensible balancing act between those two main aims of your final year: academic success and getting an appropriate job. Both of these sides of your life take time and effort, and often you'll need to be working on both concurrently. If you *know* that you're working on both effectively and efficiently, you will be far less worried that your efforts in one direction are diverting you away from what you need to achieve in the other direction.

Let's explore your confidence levels, at this moment in time. I've listed a series of bold, optimistic, confident statements in the next task. Where's your present position regarding each statement? Don't pretend to be confident if you're not yet confident. After you've tried out some of the ideas in this book, you can return to this task and see where you've *gained* confidence. That's good news. You might, however, return to the task and find that for one or two statements you've actually *lost* confidence. This is even better news, as it reflects areas where your present confidence may have been unfounded, and by then, you'll be in a stronger position to focus your efforts on such areas.

⬤ **Task: assessing your confidence**

Bold, confident statements about your present feelings, position and views	*This is very like me*	*This is quite like me*	*This is not at all like me*
1 I generally feel really optimistic about my final year, and don't foresee any problems with it.			
2 I'm determined *just* to concentrate on getting my degree, and have decided to leave getting a job till after I've got it.			
3 I've already got my job lined up for after my degree, so can devote all my energy to my studies during this final year.			
4 I'm determined to tackle job hunting just as seriously as I tackle getting a good degree during this final year.			
5 I think this final year is actually going to be *easier* than my previous years at university, as I now know how to get my act together as a student.			
6 I'm already really strategic in my approach, and have a sound final-year strategy based on tactics that I've tried and tested.			
7 I'm really good at time management, and at rationing my time so that I get everything done that I need to do.			
8 I'm really good at deciding what's urgent, and what's important, and making sure that the important things get done as well as the urgent ones.			
9 I've already perfected my revision strategy, and feel confident that it will be entirely appropriate for my final-year exams.			
10 I'm well-practised in exam technique now, and am sure that this will continue to be all I need for my final exams.			

Bold, confident statements about your present feelings, position and views	This is very like me	This is quite like me	This is not at all like me
11 Viva (oral) exams don't worry me at all, in fact I rather like the chance to tell examiners what I know.			
12 I already know that to get credit for my work (whether in exams or coursework) it is not just a matter of knowing it well, but *showing* that I know it.			
13 I am anticipating no problems with final-year assessed work, such as dissertations, essays and project write-ups.			
14 I am well-prepared to show prospective employers evidence that I have collected demonstrating that I have a wide range of important key skills.			
15 I'm good at managing my own stress levels at busy times, and know what symptoms of stress to watch out for, and how to handle them.			
16 I'm highly computer literate, and enjoy making good use of word processing, email and the Internet.			
17 I've already decided to go on to do a higher degree, and feel well-placed to seek out research opportunities.			
18 I'm looking forward to finishing my degree and getting into a job, and won't have any regrets at leaving university.			
19 I've already written a good CV, and maintain it and update it as a matter of routine.			
20 I'm well-practised at filling in job application forms, and I can do so quickly and efficiently, and make a good first impression via my forms.			

Bold, confident statements about your present feelings, position and views	This is very like me	This is quite like me	This is not at all like me
21 I'm well-practised at composing letters of application for jobs, that are special enough to get me shortlisted on most occasions.			
22 I'm not at all worried by job interviews; I am relaxed and calm, and enjoy the whole process.			
Totals			
Grand total			

That's a confident set of statements! I'd be very surprised if you ticked the 'very like me' column for all of them. Let's turn your response to the task into a confidence rating.

- Write a 'zero' beside every entry in the 'This is very like me' column.
- Write a 'one' beside each entry in the 'This is quite like me' column.
- Write a 'three' beside each entry in the 'This is not at all like me' column.
- Add up your column totals.
- Add up across the columns to get your grand total.
- If your grand total is zero, you're extremely well-prepared and confident, but perhaps have already made too many decisions, and may not see unexpected opportunities when they come along.
- If your grand total is over 66, you've counted something twice!
- The higher your score, the more this book should help you. Look now at the next version of the table, where I've put in a few pointers to other parts of this book.

Bold, confident statements about your present feelings, position and views	This is very like me	This is quite like me	This is not at all like me
1 I generally feel really optimistic about my final year, and don't foresee any problems with it.			This book should help a lot.

Bold, confident statements about your present feelings, position and views	This is very like me	This is quite like me	This is not at all like me
2 I'm determined *just* to concentrate on getting my degree, and have decided to leave getting a job till after I've got it.	Some people do this, that's fine.	You may have second thoughts on this.	Chapters 7 and 8 should help you get that job.
3 I've already got my job lined up for after my degree, so can devote all my energy to my studies during this final year.	Lucky you!	I hope it works out for you.	This book should help you do both.
4 I'm determined to tackle job hunting just as seriously as I tackle getting a good degree during this final year.	A wise decision. Chapters 7 and 8 should help.	Chapters 7 and 8 should help your job hunting to go smoothly.	OK, some people get away with leaving job hunting till later.
5 I think this final year is actually going to be *easier* than my previous years at university, as I now know how to get my act together as a student.	Some people indeed find this.	Use this book to polish your technique.	Use this book to overhaul your technique.
6 I'm already really strategic in my approach, and have a sound final-year strategy based on tactics that I've tried and tested.	Good, stay with what you've got.	Become a bit more strategic now.	Now's the time to get a real strategy, based on sound tactics.
7 I'm really good at time management, and at rationing my time so that I get everything done that I need to do.	Lucky you!	Chapters 1–4 should help.	Chapters 1–4 are bound to help – use them!
8 I'm really good at deciding what's urgent, and what's important, and making sure that the important things get done as well as the urgent ones.	Well done.	Use this book to add polish to your technique.	Use Chapters 1–4 to overhaul your task management.

Bold, confident statements about your present feelings, position and views	This is very like me	This is quite like me	This is not at all like me
9 I've already perfected my revision strategy, and feel confident that it will be entirely appropriate for my final-year exams.	Don't be *too* confident about this!	Check out Chapter 4 for further tips.	Put Chapter 4 to work for you.
10 I'm well-practised in exam technique now, and am sure that this will continue to be all I need for my final exams.	Final exams surprise some students!	Chapter 5 should help you.	Chapter 5 *will* help you!
11 Viva (oral) exams don't worry me at all, in fact I rather like the chance to tell examiners what I know.	You're fortunate.	Don't worry, see Chapters 5 and 8.	Apply parts of Chapters 5 and 8 carefully.
12 I already know that to get credit for my work (whether in exams or coursework) it is not just a matter of knowing it well, but *showing* that I know it.	A good position to be in.	Work towards showing what you know.	Work hard towards showing what you know.
13 I am anticipating no problems with final-year assessed work, such as dissertations, essays and project write-ups.	Keep it up!	Chapter 2 may have some further tips.	Put Chapter 2 to work for you.
14 I am well-prepared to show prospective employers evidence that I have collected demonstrating that I have a wide range of important key skills.	Well done, but keep collecting.	Chapter 3 could help you.	Put Chapters 1 and 3 to work for you.
15 I'm good at managing my own stress levels at busy times, and know what symptoms of	Check yourself out using the end of	Look for further polish at the end of	Overhaul your approach using the end of Chapter 1.

Bold, confident statements about your present feelings, position and views	This is very like me	This is quite like me	This is not at all like me
stress to watch out for, and how to handle them.	Chapter 1.	Chapter 1.	
16 I'm highly computer literate, and enjoy making good use of word processing, email and the Internet.	Well done.	Look for further help in Chapter 3.	Chapter 3 can help you to get started.
17 I've already decided to go on to do a higher degree, and feel well-placed to seek out research opportunities.	Fine, good luck.	Keep your options open.	This could still be an option for you.
18 I'm looking forward to finishing my degree and getting into a job, and won't have any regrets at leaving university.	That's fine, if that's what you want.	Yes, there are usually some regrets.	Glad you're enjoying it now.
19 I've already written a good CV, and maintain it and update it as a matter of routine.	Well done, keep it up.	Check out Chapter 7 for further ideas.	Put Chapter 7 to work for you.
20 I'm well-practised at filling in job application forms, and I can do so quickly and efficiently, and make a good first impression via my forms.	A good position to be in.	Use Chapter 7 to develop your technique.	Use Chapter 7 carefully, to gain a good approach.
21 I'm well-practised at composing letters of application for jobs, that are special enough to get me shortlisted on most occasions.	Keep your style up.	Improve your hit rate with Chapter 7.	It's never too late· Chapter 7 can get you going on this.
22 I'm not at all worried by job interviews; I am relaxed and calm, and enjoy the whole process.	You're fortunate.	Chapter 8 can help you.	Chapter 8 can help you a lot.

▶ Towards your final-year balancing act

If you've already got your immediate future lined up after getting your degree, the 'final-year balancing act' between your studies and preparation for your future will not apply to you. For most final-year students, however, there's a job to seek as well as exams to pass. If that's true in your case, your final year is not just about getting your degree, though that remains a central part of your agenda. The other main aspect of your final year is about what you do next. This may mean your first serious foray into the arena of job applications, writing your CV, and interviews. Much of this side of your final year will be going on alongside your studying, revising, and preparing for final exams. Tempting as it may be to say to yourself 'one thing at a time please!', the world around you doesn't work this way. This means a balancing act for you, with both of the main strands important, and at times urgent. You will need to learn to do two important things at once, making time for each, and not letting either get in the way of the other. This book is intended to help you with your final-year balancing act, so that you can mesh the two elements together smoothly and efficiently.

How should I use this book?

The short answer is: make it *work* for you, don't just read it! What you get out of using this book is up to you. In that respect, this book is no different to any of the main subject-material sources you will be using to prepare for your final exams. It's what you *do* with the ideas in this (or any) book that counts. The best ideas in the world won't do you any good if you just read about them, and nod to yourself and say 'oh yes, that's sensible'. You need to adjust what you do to take on board those ideas that are relevant to you. Here are three ways you can put this book to work for you.

- **Write all over it!** Provided, of course, that it's *your* book, and not a library copy! When you see a suggestion that triggers an action point for you, jot it down on the page. If you make a habit of this, before long the book will be full of your own good intentions. What *you* write will be more important than my words.
- **Look for tactics to turn into your strategy.** Tactics are about *what* to do, *how* to do it, and *when* to do it. You'll need hundreds of tactics to make your final year successful, efficient and enjoyable. A strategy is an organized collection of tactics. There's got to be a good answer to the question *'why?'* (as well as to the questions 'what?', 'how?' and 'when?') to justify selecting the tactics that will make up your strategy. The best

answer to the question 'why?' is: because you've proved that a tactic works for you, so . . .

- **Try things out straightaway.** When you find an idea that makes sense to you, do something about it there and then. Test it out. Find out whether it works for you. There's no point in your reading this book and becoming very *knowledgeable* about how to tackle your final year. You won't get an award for this kind of knowledge. The prizes come from *applying* the knowledge.

My suggestions about using this book may well apply to many of the other books, articles, handouts and resources that you'll be using for your final-year studies. Try to adopt the position that all of your resources are to be *used*, not just read.

You're way past the time when you could have the luxury of reading about study techniques just for fun. You're now in a long, continuous exam, which contains all those other exams, and your preparations for them. This long exam also contains all those other things such as sorting out your career, developing yourself into someone who will be a success-ful candidate at interviews, and so on. Use this book as a companion during this long exam. Take from it what works for you. Use it to remind yourself of the big picture. Use it to help you choose tactics to deal with the small pixels of that big picture.

1 ☀ Time to be strategic!

▶ Setting your sights

If you know where you're going, you're much more likely to get there. It's not much use just plodding along a familiar pathway when you're heading for somewhere definite that you've not reached before. That's why, during your final year, you need to set your sights on the degree you wish to gain. It's tempting, however, to do all sorts of things instead of working steadily towards that degree. It can feel comforting to pretend that the vital stages of your final year are still a very long way off. You may feel like immersing yourself in the minutiae of the tasks that you're immediately involved with. You may hope that, as long as you're doing *some* work towards your degree, this will be enough. It's easy to postpone the decision to really start working towards your degree, and just attend to the bits and pieces which make up your present coursework. Lots of students work really *hard* during their final year, but fewer work *smart*. If you're working hard, make sure that you're working on the *real* business of being a final-year student, and not just on all the other kinds of hard work that you're surrounded by.

It's useful to think about what sort of degree you're really aiming for. In the UK, you may be working within a degree classification system, where there's a possibility of getting a first-class degree, or an upper second-class degree, or a lower second-class degree, or even a third-class degree or a pass degree. If you're aiming for a first-class degree, you'll either be the sort of student who is already well on the way to getting it, or you'll be pulling out all of the stops in your final year to maximize your performance in exams and other assessment elements which count in degree classification.

What do you have to do differently to get a first-class degree? There's no simple answer to this question, other than 'a bit more' or even 'a lot more' than someone who gets a second-class degree. Lecturers often say that they can spot who's likely to be heading for a first-class degree from the extra flair they demonstrate at coursework, and the keener interest they show in the subjects they're studying. Perhaps the most significant single factor that gets people good degrees is consistency. There's no room for a weak subject if you're aiming for a good degree, which means that it's worth setting out quite deliberately to balance out your work so that you give a good performance in everything you do during your final-year studies. You might find that the tactics I suggested in another Open University Press study guide (Race 1999) will help you to decide how to 'study smart' in the academic side of your life, and the present book may then help you to 'apply smart' when you come to start seriously on your job-hunting activities.

Most students achieve second-class degrees. An upper second-class degree is not as good as a first-class degree in terms of getting you to the top of shortlists when you go job hunting, or for opening up opportunities to do research and study for higher degrees. However, most people with upper second-class degrees can go on to research if they really want to. Many people that I know with lower second-class degrees wish very much now that they had at least an upper second-class one! A little strategic help in their final year might have gone a long way. A third-class degree is still a degree, and will still give you letters to put beside your name. Sooner or later, however, employers and others tend to ask what sort of degree you have, and then you will wish you had something better.

You may indeed have already decided that you're not aiming to be at the top of the pass list, and that you just want to make sure you get a reasonable degree, without putting your whole being into striving for a first-class one. You may even have become convinced that you're not up to competing with some of your fellow students, who seem always to find things easy which you find hard. However, it's not just a matter of intelligence or application – technique comes into the picture too. The ideas in this book are intended to help you improve your technique during your final year, so that it does not let you down.

▶ Changing your study habits

You will need to change your study habits for your final year. This is both good news and bad news. The bad news is that any kind of change takes some time and needs some planning. The good news is that the sort of changes that will help you make your final year successful will also help you to make it a year which is more effective, more efficient and more enjoyable.

Think back to your first year at university. You probably remember working really hard, and the feeling that you had a lot on your plate at the time. Some subjects may have been entirely new. Sometimes, you may have found yourself behind some of your fellow students, who seemed to have covered topics that you'd never come across. You may also have had a lot of adjustments to make in your life in general, such as finding somewhere suitable to live, making new friends and struggling to maintain contact with old ones. That first year may have been quite an uphill struggle at times, as you learned to find your way round how university education works.

In your second year at university, you may have found it all got easier. You may have found that you could almost coast along, and spare a lot more time for all the other things you were interested in besides keeping up with your studies. The final hurdle, your final year, may have seemed a comfortable way off. Plenty of time.

Then, quite suddenly you may have realized that your final year is upon you. The hurdle is no longer the final year as a whole, but (for example), those crucial exams looming up at the end of that final year, or perhaps that important research project, or dissertation. The fact that the hurdle is better defined now can cause some stomach churning, and lead you into the temptation to escape from the tension that results by avoiding thinking about it!

You've only got your final year once. Of course, it's not as black and white as this – there are usually second chances, such as repeating the year, or doing some resit exams if you find yourself down in one or two subjects. You may, however, only have one chance to get a *good* degree. And think of the tension of having to repeat things that you've failed once already. All in all, it's well worth resolving to make a good run at your final year, and to change your lifestyle, temporarily, to maximize your chance of success and safeguard the outcome. It's not a lot of good changing your lifestyle just a few weeks before your final exams. You'll need to work hard then anyway. As I suggested earlier, it's not really a matter of just working hard, it's about working smart. The smart decision is to take on your final year with a different spirit than that which might have been quite OK in the middle year (or years) of your time at university.

What about all those other things in your life?

The short answer is 'task management'. You may well have all sorts of other things going on in your life besides studying. You may be working part-time to support yourself through your studies. You may indeed be working full-time, and trying to do as much, as a part-time student, as is expected of full-time students working towards the same degree as you. You may have by now a lot of friends at your university. Relationships may now be more serious. You may have family responsibilities. What happens if something unexpected occurs – for example family illness at home, and so on? You can't cut yourself off entirely from all the rest of the world while you work through your final year. Even if you could, that would not mean that your work towards your degree would be guaranteed successful.

The most sensible solution is to keep everything else in your life going, but at reduced power. Spend a little less time on everything, except:

- *organizing* your final year – selecting the tactics that will help you both to be successful academically, and to develop your attractiveness to potential employers or research supervisors;
- *implementing* your tactics and turning them into a coherent strategy to make your final year a time of efficiency and effectiveness in everything it entails;
- *safeguarding* yourself, making sure that you don't put yourself under unreasonable pressure, which could damage your success.

▶ What are your enemies?

If you're now a final-year student, you're still there! You haven't withdrawn. You're not a 'non-completer'. Mantz Yorke (1999) recently published an analysis of the principal causes of students giving up, entitled *Leaving Early: Undergraduate Non-Completion in Higher Education*. This includes a survey of the influences reported by 2151 full-time (and sandwich course) students, as reasons why they quit higher education. If you were going to quit, you probably would have done so already, but it's useful to look through some of the principal causes, as during your final year some of them may still influence you:

- 39 per cent of students who gave up reported that they *chose the wrong field of study*. Sometimes you'll feel that way too. However, in your final year, it's best to stay with what you've chosen, not least because it just takes too much energy to start all over again in a different discipline area.
- Almost as many (38 per cent) reported that '*lack of commitment to the programme*' had a moderate or considerable influence on their decision to throw in the towel. This may partly be the fault of the course, but also reflects their own motivation and commitment. If at times you feel a similar lack of commitment, the main thing to remember is that it's your *final* year – you don't have to maintain that commitment for much longer.
- 37 per cent of non-completers reported that *financial problems* had a moderate or considerable influence on their decision. That's not surprising. But if you've survived financial problems until now, it would

be sad to let such problems be the cause of not quite getting to the end of your final year.

- The same number of students (37 per cent) quit because the programme was *'not what I expected'*. Now that you're in your final year, you are likely to have adjusted your expectations, and be content with your course.
- 31 per cent reported that *'the teaching did not suit me'*. Most students, however, who don't enjoy the teaching on their courses, find out about this long before their final year. Therefore, during your final year it's unlikely to be the last straw for you. In fact, during your final year, the quality or nature of the teaching you experience is unlikely to be a particularly important factor, as what counts is your *learning*. Much of this you will be doing independently. Also, final-year classes tend to be much smaller than (for example) first-year ones, and as a result students tend to find the teaching more acceptable.
- 30 per cent said that *'insufficient academic progress'* was a reason influencing their decision to drop out. You may well sympathize with them at times during your final year, but you've already progressed enough to be there in the first place, so this should not be something that really gets you down.
- 28 per cent reported that they *'needed a break from education'*. In your final year, you've got a break (or at least a major change) coming up quite shortly, so if there are days when you feel like a break, don't make it a permanent one by dropping out!

There are other dangers too. *'Emotional difficulties with others'* and *'personal health problems'* were cited by 23 per cent of students who quit as having a moderate or considerable influence on their decision. These factors *can* continue into your final year. That's partly why you need to be strategic, and to look after yourself. Similarly, 22 per cent cited *'stress related to the programme'* as a reason for leaving. This stress is likely to go up, if anything, during your final year, so again you need to be taking good care of yourself. All of these factors are related to balancing your act during your final year, and this book is designed to help you strike a sensible balance.

There are many other 'enemies'. Mantz Yorke's (1999) survey includes factors such as:

- lack of study skills;
- accommodation problems;
- needs of dependants;
- travel difficulties;
- homesickness;
- demands of employment while studying;
- problems with drugs or alcohol;
- bereavement of someone close;
- pregnancy (self or partner's).

Any of these can be very real problems. Any of them can be enough to put you off your stride in your final year. Some of these problems are quite beyond your control. Take comfort, however, in the fact that they're statistically far less likely than some of the enemies referred to earlier. For most of these problems, far less than 20 per cent of the students who quit cited them as contributory factors. And if you were to have had serious accommodation, travel or homesickness problems, you are likely to have worked out suitable compromises already.

If you're a part-time final-year student, some things are quite different. In a survey of 328 part-time students who withdrew from their courses, over half said that *'demands of employment while studying'* had a moderate or considerable influence on their decision to leave. A quarter cited *'needs of dependants'* or *'workload too heavy'* as contributory factors. Far fewer mentioned a lack of commitment to the programme.

If you're a full-time final-year student tempted to quit, get a job, then return as a part-timer, it's worth noting that some of the potential problems are eased as a result, but that others (demands of employment while studying) obviously get much worse.

However, there's a twist in the tale of the 2151 students who withdrew. Of them, 53 per cent had already returned to study in higher education by the time their responses were analysed, with another 20 per cent intending to do so. The moral of this is that even if you're sorely tempted, on some of the darkest days of your final year, to escape from your degree programme altogether, you're more than likely to be back quite soon! Therefore, grit your teeth and save yourself a lot of additional work, worry and stress, and stay with it for that little bit longer. Reappraise your toolkit of tactics, re-plan your strategy and get on with tackling your final year, not digging your escape tunnel to yet another final year on the other side.

Working out what counts most, and building your own motivation

Nothing improves motivation more than the feeling of being ahead of yourself, and staying ahead of yourself. Think of the opposite scenario: what if you're really lagging behind in your final year? Everything then seems like a battle. Each new task seems like a conspiracy to stop you from catching up. Anything unexpected seems like a disaster.

Getting ahead means working out very systematically and logically where to spend your time and energy. There's not a lot of point spending hours polishing up something at which you're already very good. It is very *comforting* to spend most of your time on things you're good at, but you may only gain a few marks in your final exams for this. It's much more important to spend most of your energy on things that will gain you a lot more credit. There is more credit to be gained by systematically attacking your known weaknesses. This is not so comfortable, but it brings its own kind of motivation. When you *know* you're doing something that is going to improve your opportunities, it's easier to put more time and effort into your work. Think in terms of 'learning pay-off'; more about this next.

▶ Maximizing your learning pay-off

Your final year is the time to be quite strategic. If you're doing something with a high learning pay-off, you're winning. If you're spending ages on something, but not learning much in the process, you should consider changing tactics.

What is 'learning pay-off' anyway? Probably the best way to think of it is like this: contribution, per hour spent, towards gaining your degree, *and* getting your act together for the next part of your life. Let's look randomly at some of the activities you'll do in your final year, and see which of them deliver high (or low) learning pay-off as defined here.

- **Copying down notes in lectures, from what you see on the board or screen, or transcribing directly things a lecturer says.** This tends to have low learning pay-off, because you can do it without really thinking about it. You will do better by trying to make your own notes, based on what you see and hear; this helps you to begin *learning* about it.
- **Copying out bits and pieces from journal articles and textbooks into essays (duly acknowledged, of course).** Low learning pay-off again. It is better to keep your quotations short, and to make your own comments *about* each extract you use.
- **Writing out (or typing out) the eighth draft of an essay or report.** This may get you slightly better marks than the seventh draft would, but may take far too long to be worth the extra reward.
- **Looking back over a set of lecture notes for a few lectures, and spending an hour writing down 107 short, sharp questions which you will aim to become able to answer about the content of those lectures.** This has high learning pay-off, as it gets you thinking critically about what *you* have to do with the content, and it provides you with a *tool* to help you become able to deliver on what you're learning.
- **Deciding what the standards of your forthcoming exams are by analysing past questions critically, and working out exactly what you would need to be able to do to answer them well.** This has high learning pay-off, as it helps you to tune yourself in to the assessment standards and the culture of the assessment system within which you will be working.

- **Writing a list of questions that you can't yet answer (whether from your lecture notes or from reference sources)**. Provided you keep a keen eye on your published syllabus and on any information you can glean about the assessment criteria you're working towards, this can have high learning pay-off. If you know what your questions are, you can ask people (lecturers and/or fellow students) till you find out the answers. Alternatively, you can look up the answers in further source materials.
- **Looking regularly (and quickly) at the advertisements for the kind of jobs for which you think you will be applying**. This can have high learning pay-off towards the overall success of your final year, by familiarizing you with the field you're planning to enter, and reducing the time you will need to spend on job hunting when pressures of studying become higher.
- **Making a very rough draft of bits and pieces which will go into any final year dissertation you may have to write**. This has high learning pay-off, as the earlier you start on it, the more time you have to polish it (and polishing takes far less time and energy than starting).
- **Preparing a draft of your CV really early, and getting as many people's feedback on it as you can**. This can have high learning pay-off, and means you will only need to make relatively slight adjustments to your CV when you need it – particularly useful at times when other pressures such as revision may be present.
- **Practising on some 'dummy' application forms, of the sort that you're soon going to be filling out for real**. This can have high learning pay-off, especially if you get feedback from other people on what they think of your draft applications. You will be learning to tackle application forms better, and more efficiently, and this will pay dividends when you're doing applications alongside concentrated studying.
- **Working *with* fellow students, rather than against them**. This can have high learning pay-off, as you'll learn a lot by explaining things to them, and will be practising explaining those things for real in your final examinations.

▶ Managing your time for a much-increased workload

The most common reason that people give for not having done anything as well as they could have done it is that they didn't have enough time. In fact, that's often not the *real* reason. All final-year students have the same amount of time in their final year – one year! Or at least, parts of one year (those parts of the year that are in their control). That's where the secret lies: taking more control of the time that you have. The suggestions in the following task on time management are all just plain common sense, but the problem is that common sense tends to go out of the window when human beings become under pressure or stressed, and this just makes things worse.

 Task: assessing your time management skills

Tick each of the suggestions below that you *know* you are already putting into practice, and put a star beside those that you could improve, and a few stars beside any suggestion that could make a big difference to your time management.

- **Distinguish between what's important and what's urgent**. We all tend to feel under pressure to do urgent tasks. This can mean that important tasks get left undone, and guess what? They become the next urgent ones. Tackling your final year well depends on doing the important tasks as well as you can. If you've got an urgent task to do, do a non-urgent but important one *first*, at least for ten minutes. You'll then have made a start on something important, and the urgent task will still get done – ten minutes won't make much difference to that.

- **Make yourself 'to-do lists'.** I still do this – I find it's a good habit for life in general, let alone studying. You might find it useful to make a grid with columns, like this:

Date	Urgency	Task and action needed	Date done

You may be surprised how much better it feels just to make that list. Once the tasks are out of your head and onto the list, they don't seem so daunting. Sometimes there are fewer tasks than you think. It gives you a good sense of achievement to tick off a task you've just finished. When there's not a lot of time, choose a small task, do it, and tick it off. When there's more time, start a longer one, and half-tick it.

- Use the *first* **10 per cent of any available time.** You will know how, left to human nature, we usually do most things in the last 10 per cent of the available time. And we usually do them just about well enough, even then. It stands to reason that we could do them just as well in the *first* 10 per cent of the available time. Then, we could return to them now and then during the rest of the available time, and polish them, and make them even better.

- **Ration your time according to the learning pay-off you're getting from it.** If you find that certain tasks are taking a long time, and not delivering learning pay-off, cut them short. Don't spend too long, for example, chasing the last few per cent of the marks available for an item of coursework, when your final exams are looming up. You'd be better off getting slightly less marks for the coursework, and ensuring that you pass the exams well.

- **Try to do *all* of your coursework tasks reasonably well, rather than just *some* of them very well.** (Ignore this if you *know* that only the best few will be counted towards your degree.) Too many students end up with gaps in their coursework profile, often because they spent too long on certain elements, and did not leave themselves time to submit others. If you fail to submit an element of coursework, you'll get exactly 0 per cent for it! Even if you submit a rather sketchy essay, or a rather poorly structured report, and so on, you'll get significantly more than 0 per cent: you're more likely to get as much as 40 per cent, or a bare pass.

- **Match effort to potential reward.** For example, if your final exams count for 50 per cent, and your total coursework also counts for 50 per cent, don't spend more than half your time attending to coursework. Use half of your available study time to prepare for the exams, all the way from now till then. That may mean doing some coursework a little less thoroughly than you could have done, but will not make all that much difference to your coursework marks (provided you take note of the previous point as well of course).

- **Don't expect to study for 24 hours a day, seven days a week!** That's not what time management is about. Take into account your own concentration spans. If you work best for 20 minutes at a time, rather than two hours at a time, get in lots and lots of 20-minute spells of study. Take breaks. Do something completely different, to give your brain a rest. Even while 'resting', your brain will still be making sense, subconsciously, of the things you were thinking about in the last 20 minutes. This process of making sense of what you've been learning is every bit as important as when you were consciously trying to learn it.

- **Don't overestimate what you can do in a whole clear day.** Sometimes, we feel 'if only I had an uninterrupted day to catch up with all of those things to do which are cluttering my brain'. When such a day comes, we only get through some of them. Any whole day needs to include rests! And some tasks take longer than expected.

- **Manage your distractions.** You may be able to turn some of your distractions into reward systems instead. For example, you can *earn* for yourself such rewards as watching a favourite TV programme, or going out with friends, or watching a movie, or even eating chocolates or drinking beer! Don't be *too* kind to yourself however!

Forget your (mental) exercise bike: cycle purposefully towards your degree and your new life

An exercise bike can be really good for helping you to get fit, but it doesn't actually take you anywhere. It's better, in the context of studying and working towards your first postgraduate job, to get fit by getting somewhere. Don't just exercise; *do* things that are directly relevant to your studying and your future career. You'll get just as fit as you might have done by simply exercising your brain, and there will be tangible results which don't just apply to tackling your final year.

How long can you work really hard? How long can you devote your life to studying and very little else? Do you actually *need* to let study take over your life completely during your final year? And if you did do this, would it actually be wise?

You know that your final year counts for a lot. Your final qualification is in the balance. So is your first postgraduate job. You are aiming to achieve both. You are aiming to do as well as you can in your efforts to achieve both. This does not, however, mean you've got to put your entire body and mind into top gear and pedal relentlessly towards your dual targets. You want to reach your targets, but not to drop by the wayside, exhausted, *en route*. You need to save energy for the really important parts of your journey, such as your final exams and those crucial job interviews. If you're exhausted, you won't do yourself justice in either of these. Pace yourself. Set your sights, and keep up your momentum, but at a sustainable pace.

▶ Getting credit for your learning: showing what you know

You've done quite enough by now to know a lot about how the assessment system works. You don't actually get credit for what you know, you get credit for what you *show* that you know. All of the marks which contribute towards your degree are for things that you've produced as *evidence* of what you know. You may know ten times as much as you ever show, but you can't get any credit for the difference.

The same will apply when you make job applications. The credit you get is for what you *show* about yourself on your CV and on your application forms and letters of application, and at interview. You don't actually get credit for being a wonderful potential employee unless you can *show* that you're such a person.

A wise tactic for your final year is to concentrate on showing rather than knowing. The knowing will take care of itself if you consciously develop your technique of showing what you know, showing what you are, showing what you can do, and showing what you can be.

'Working in captivity'

In your final year, there are so many things to do! Wouldn't it be easier if you didn't have:

- lectures to attend;
- tutorials to go to;
- seminars to attend, perhaps one to prepare and present;
- practical work to do and write up;
- that field trip to go on;
- that independent study package to work through, and so on.

You probably won't have all of these, but the problem is that time that is beyond your direct control feels very threatening when you've got so many things to squeeze into the time that *is* in your control. Imagine yourself sitting in a rather boring lecture, thinking 'I don't want to be here now. I've got better things to do with my time right now. I'd be better off spending this hour on such-and-such, which is far more import-ant than what's going on at this lecture! I've got that application form to fill in before tomorrow anyway'.

You may indeed decide to cut some losses. It is quite logical to pick one or two topics and decide for yourself that 'This would not be worth me spending any more time on at this stage in the game. I can manage without answering any exam questions on this. I will make sure that I've still got sufficient choice in the exam, and concentrate on my strengths now'. However, this strategy can be risky. The questions which remain may not be ideal ones for you. The boring (or difficult) subject may, with a little effort and investment of time, turn out to be better for you than some of your presently-preferred choices. The best advice I can offer you is quite simple: put your time 'in captivity' to good use. In other words, when your time is not your own, get the most you can from every minute of it.

In lectures, or tutorials, or seminars on your preferred topics, *think* deep. Don't just *take* notes in lectures, *make* notes. Copying things down from the screen, board, or from what a lecturer says is not exercising your mind, and you'll learn little from the process. Even just putting the same things down in your own words, in your own way, gets your mind working, and has a much higher learning pay-off. In your final-year classes, keep asking yourself 'Is this bit really important?', 'Is this something I should prepare to be able to write about in answer to exam questions?', and 'What are the most central points to remember here?'. As you *make* your notes, make sure that next time you glance at these notes, the answers to those three questions spring from your pages as written.

When sitting in lectures, seminars, tutorials and so on, keep reminding yourself that you're in the presence of the people who have already designed your final exam questions. Final-year questions have to be set a considerable time in advance of your exams, so that they can be vetted by external examiners. Your lecturers and tutors are also the people who will constitute the final exam board. Tune in to how they think. The better you can do this, the better you will be able to satisfy them with your answers to their questions.

Also, keep an eye on your competition. In any situations where you're with other students, monitor how they're getting on with their final year. You'll often be alerted to something that it would be useful for *you* to think about too. More often, you may be alerted to how you're ahead of the game, and that's good for your confidence. Use any opportunity you have to explain things that *you* understand to fellow students who don't yet understand them. This is not worsening your position in the final-year race – it's well proven that the person who explains things deepens their own learning much more than the person who receives the explanation. The things that other students can't understand may well be exactly those things which you really *need* to have a good grip on. The act of explaining strengthens that grip.

In short, don't just spend your time 'in captivity' passively receiving information, with half your mind elsewhere. Actively *process* the information, and think *behind* it. Take control of your mind, and use it to extract all the clues you can about what you need to become able to deliver. Play detective. Even in the most boring lectures you can keep control of your brain, *and* keep it active. If there's really nothing of any significance whatsoever going on in the lecture, and no clues to tune in to, you can always be *thinking* about something else important. Have some lists of questions about other subjects with you in any case, and when there's nothing better to do, exercise your mind on these. You don't have to stop your revising just because you're in a class!

Covering your back: making up for any earlier deficits in scores and grades

Lots of students don't work as hard as they could have done in their penultimate year. They often say how they now wish that they'd put a great deal more into that penultimate year. They enter their final year with weak areas which have been diagnosed (and recorded) in earlier assessments and exams.

Some of such assessments may still count a little towards your final qualification. However, when you know what the problems were, you can set out to prove during your final year that you've entirely overcome them. Don't just try to put earlier problems to the back of your mind, set out to *show* that you've now rectified them. At the final exam board, when your academic record is reviewed, work towards someone being able to say on your behalf 'Candidate X seemed to have difficulties with topic Y during the previous year, but final-year performance shows that this has been entirely resolved'.

▶ Cultivating your final-year cultures

There are three main cultures which you will need to address during your final year. They are:

- The *assessment* culture, which determines how you will need to demonstrate your mastery of the subjects you are studying.
- The *career development* culture, which is about the sorts of things that employers will be looking for as you put yourself onto the job market.
- The *research* culture, which you will be wise to investigate anyway, so that you keep your options open to continue to postgraduate work, even if you're presently not even considering it. If, of course, you're already determined to continue on to research, you'll probably be tuning yourself in to the research culture in your discipline all the time, by reading, observing researchers at your own institution, and so on.

Each of these cultures will be specific to your own subject discipline area, and you will need to use your wits to tune in to them. The best way to tune in to what's required in each of these three aspects, in *your* discipline area, is to pose to yourself questions such as those below, and act on the answers you find. These answers are going to be an important basis for the ground-rules for your final year.

Assessment culture

This is how to cut to the chase in the academic side of your final year – find out as much as you can about the assessment culture. Don't just regard it as something that's going to happen to you whether you like it or not. It may be outside your control, but it's well within your practice zone. For each of the questions below, remember the two maxims underpinning this book: 'How can I work *smart* to prepare myself for each and every form of assessment?' and 'How best can I practise to *show* what I know?'.

 Task: what do you know about your assessment culture?

Check out how much you know about the assessment culture you're working in by jotting down your own immediate short answers to the list of questions below, and noting which questions you do not yet have answers to.

1 What is the balance between continuous or coursework assessment, and exam-type assessment?
   • Entirely coursework?
   • Some coursework, but mainly exam?
   • About 50:50 coursework and exam?
   • Mostly exam?
   • Entirely exam?
   • Exam plus one significant element of coursework, for example a dissertation or project?
   • A different combination from any of the above?

2 What kinds of exam are you likely to meet in your discipline area?
   • Time-constrained unseen written exams (for example two or three hours, where you don't know any of the questions in advance)?
   • Time-constrained open-book exams (where you can take in any – or specified – resource materials, and use them to answer the exam questions)?
   • Time-constrained open-notes exams (where you can take in your own notes, but not published materials or books)?
   • Oral exams?
   • Practical exams?
   • Other forms of exam, such as time-unconstrained exams (where you have some choice over how long you spend answering the questions)?

3 Which of the following types of question or task dominates the continuous assessment on your course?
   • Essays?
   • Quantitative problems?
   • Qualitative problems?
   • Case studies?
   • Practical reports?
   • Studio work?
   • Other types of assessment?

4 Which of the following types of exam question are most usual in your discipline?
  • Long essays, for example two or three in three hours?
  • Shorter essays, for example more than three in three hours?
  • Long quantitative problems, an hour or more each?
  • Shorter quantitative problems, for example half an hour each?
  • Answers based on case study data supplied in the exam?
  • Decision-making exercises under exam conditions?
  • Short-answer exam questions?
  • Multiple-choice exam questions?
  • Other types of exam assessment?

Career development culture

What will be the main factors to impress potential employers in your discipline? Several of the factors listed below may apply to your discipline. Try to rank them in order of importance.

• Your academic record, for example degree classification?
• Evidence of your work, such as in a portfolio?
• Reports from your referees?
• Your performance at formal interviews?
• Your performance at informal interviews?
• Your performance at specific tests, for example psychometric tests?

I've included much more detail on job hunting later in this book.

Research culture

In different disciplines, there are ways of balancing your tactics to create a systematic strategy for making yourself an attractive proposition to potential research supervisors, and get funding for postgraduate research. Check which of the following are most likely to apply to your own position, if you are considering the option of going on to research.

• Will it be up to you to decide upon a research topic, and to find yourself a supervisor?
• Will you be wanting to identify a potential supervisor at your own institution, or somewhere else?
• Will it be up to you to make yourself a good proposition for a research supervisor, but where the main idea for a research proposal may stem from the supervisor rather than from you?
• May you find yourself in the position of having to choose between several potential research supervisors, all with fairly definite research topics in mind?

- Will potential research supervisors be influenced mainly by your academic qualifications, or will their existing knowledge of you as a person come into the picture?
- Will possible research supervisors be strongly influenced by other people's opinions of your potential for research?

Having reached your final year, you may not have realized just how much information you have picked up on the way about the three cultures outlined above. However, much of this information may have been subconscious. The purpose of my questions was to bring the answers into your conscious mind, so that you can use them, and from them continue to develop your final-year strategy.

▶ Adjusting your attitudes to lecturers and tutors

During your first year, you may have been part of a large group of students, and may not have had any real chance to get to know many of your lecturers. Later on in your course, you may have had more opportunity to build links with at least some of the staff in your university. It's important to use your final year to develop and consolidate such links, particularly if you're planning to continue towards postgraduate research. You may be hoping to be considered as a good research student prospect by one or more of your lecturers or tutors. You may also need them as referees for your job applications, or for applications to do research at a different university.

Be more forthcoming at tutorials, for example, to show your tutors that you're interested, alert and keen. Don't be a thorn in their sides. Be constructive. Don't monopolize the tutorials. Be seen to be considerate to fellow students. Aim to make a good impression. Aim to get your tutors to like you! This is good practice for aiming to get potential employers to 'like' you from what they see of you at future interviews.

Don't forget, above all, that it's the lecturers and tutors that you encounter during your final year who will be your assessors for your most important exams. They may know you better than you think – final-year classes are smaller, there's less chance for you to just be a face in the crowd any more. Final-year marking may well be 'anonymous', but lecturers can often tell whose work they are marking. They may know your handwriting rather well! And even if the final-year marking is really anonymous, and no subjectivity creeps into your assessment, the exam board at the end of it all won't be anonymous. Candidates are considered by name. If you're on a borderline, your lecturers will discuss whether you deserve to be moved up – or even down. Their attitudes to you are very important.

'It's just not fair!'

What should you do if there are things you're really not happy about during your final year? Life isn't fair, and your final year is bound to have its share of injustices. The biggest danger is that because you're under more pressure in your final year, and because more is at stake, you could overreact to injustices and difficult circumstances.

Some of the things that could go wrong with your final year, through no fault of your own, include:

- Your course leader leaves the university to go somewhere else, and there's no one sufficiently experienced in the specialism that was taught by this member of staff to finish off the teaching associated with the exam questions that have already been put into the system.
- Dr Podsworthy always *was* one of your worst lecturers, but now you're in your final year, and one of your exam papers is his, you feel that your whole degree could be in jeopardy because of his bad teaching!
- The department has a teaching quality review visit halfway through your final year, and all of the staff are busy getting their act together so that all the paperwork and systems will be impeccable on the week of the visit, and the teaching itself on that week will be spectacularly brilliant. As a result, in the weeks or months during the run-up to the visit, none of the staff seem to have time for teaching, or students, or anything else!
- A big change in the course structure happens during your final year. The university switches from terms to semesters, or back from semesters to terms, or course structures are modularized. Your cohort feel like guinea pigs, and indeed you might be.
- There's a move into a new (or different) building, and staff and students alike waste a lot of time and energy just getting themselves organized – why did it have to happen during *your* final year?
- There's a restructuring of the university, or a merger with another institution, and all of the senior staff seem to be playing politics, and jostling for the best posts in the new situation, and you feel that you're not getting as much of their attention as you need in your final year.

The scenarios above all have one thing in common: other people's actions could affect *your* degree. That's not fair. You've got a right to complain. There's the 'Student Charter' that your university is so proud of. There's the policy of having student representatives on course committees. The Students' Union could help sort it all out, but probably not in time to help *you* in your final year. However much anyone makes a fuss about any of the scenarios above, they're not going to go away. If they're going to affect the quality of teaching and support that you get in your final year, that effect will still happen, however loudly anyone complains.

Complaining and seeking justice may be your right, but it is a stressful business. You've got enough stress in your final year without looking for more. Even though you think it will give you great satisfaction to pursue Dr Podsworthy towards dismissal for appalling teaching, you're very unlikely to win such campaigns – he's more likely to be promoted to where his poor teaching does less damage! If serious charges are levelled against a community of bright people (don't forget that your lecturers *are* bright), they tend to unite and bury their differences, and set up a robust defence against the charges. And the power is loaded in their favour – don't forget they set and mark *your* exams, and some of them will be the people you need to write *your* references, and so on.

In your *first* year at university it may have been worth your time and energy to be a campaigner for student rights, and a seeker after fairness and equity. In your final year, why you? If you divert your own energy to such things, you could be robbing yourself. You could be singling yourself out as a troublemaker.

Put it into perspective. Most of the institutional problems in the list above won't just affect you, they'll affect your cohort. If everyone's performance is down in a final exam, that in itself will be enough proof that something was wrong, and staff will be brought to account, or marks will be moderated upwards in consultation with external examiners. It's worth keeping your own personal log of any circumstances beyond your control on which you might want to draw in the event of you lodging an appeal against one of your own final-year results. At least, then, no one would be influenced by your dissatisfaction at the moment of assessing your work. Don't overestimate appeals anyway. Think how academics are likely to feel when anyone appeals against their judgement. They (like anyone else) are looking for vindication of their professional integrity. If something really *has* gone seriously wrong, an appeal may sort it out, but if things have only gone *slightly* wrong, an appeal is likely to cause them to dig themselves into their position and defend themselves.

In short, my advice is 'don't make waves'. Your final year is not the best time for this. It takes too much of *your* energy to generate waves. To be cynical, if the problem's really bad, it's likely that someone else will make the waves anyway! Remember that it's *your* final year. Save your energy for all the things you *can* do something about, such as writing a really good dissertation, revising well, polishing your exam technique, and making yourself an attractive proposition to employers. In all of these, it's *your* game, and you can win it.

▶ Gathering evidence

Your final year is your most important opportunity to keep your options open. It is a time to be opening up alternative possibilities. Even if you have a very good idea now about what you plan to do immediately after you get your degree, it is useful to have some alternative pathways lined up. One or more of these alternatives may actually prove to be much more interesting and attractive than your present plans. You may find that however keen you are on your present plans, things could turn out such that they just aren't going to be an option for you. Someone else may get there first.

What you need is *evidence*. You don't just need evidence of your academic strengths; your degree itself will be taken as the most reliable evidence of these. You need additional evidence of your personal strengths. You will need to show potential employers that you're a notch above fellow applicants for the posts for which you apply. You may need to show potential research supervisors that you've got just a little more going for you than have the other students who want to go on to research.

What sorts of evidence do you need? For a start, you need to be able to demonstrate that you're a good communicator. People like good communicators. That doesn't mean monopolizing every oral communication occasion; good communicators need to show well-developed *listening* skills as well as being able to get their points across when required. We all try, when necessary, to accommodate people who are 'hard of hearing', but just think for a moment of someone who is 'hard of listening' – that's a more serious problem for some!

You also need to have evidence that you're good at written communication. This doesn't just mean in the exam room, or writing essays and reports. If you've written for a newspaper, or a magazine, that may show that you can communicate well in writing in non-academic circumstances as well as in academic ones. If you've done the paperwork for a committee or student society, you'll have a lot of evidence to draw on to show that you're not just an expert at academic writing.

If you're studying in such disciplines as art and design you will need to be able to show future employers (or potential research supervisors) your creative potential. You will need to have accumulated a representative portfolio of your work, which you can take to them, and talk through with them. Many of the elements of such a portfolio may arise from set coursework during your final year, but there's no need to limit your own personal portfolio to things that you have been *required* to do as part of your course. Indeed, the *extra* elements that distinguish your portfolio from those of other applicants may be the most significant ones when people make their decisions about *your* future.

In Chapter 3, we return in more detail to the business of assembling your evidence, this time linking evidence to the skills that you will be developing during your final year. Some of these skills will be study-related, but many others go far wider than that. Let's end this 'Time to be strategic' chapter with a strategic look at stress!

▶ Managing your own stress levels

There's a great deal of talk about stress these days. There are many colourful terms in everyday usage, cheering terms such as 'burn-out', 'road rage', 'stress-related illness'. It is now acknowledged that consistent, long-term stress damages our bodies, increasing the risk of heart problems, strokes and infection. It is now claimed that recent discoveries about stress-related physical illness are among the most significant breakthroughs in medical research since smoking and cancer were first linked 40 years ago.

⦿ **Task: assessing your stress level**

Let's see how stressed you are at the present moment, then we'll see what we can do about it (if indeed you turn out to be stressed, of course). Answer the following questions.

Possible feelings about stress, and reactions to causes of stress: only tick one column for each factor listed below	*This is me!*	*This is a bit like me*	*This isn't me at all*
1 I simply feel very stressed!			
2 I'm frightened that I may now be stressed.			
3 I'm frightened that I may become stressed during my final year.			
4 I don't know what will happen to me if I get stressed.			
5 I can't sleep at night.			
6 My heart rate is often abnormally raised.			
7 I often suffer from dizziness.			
8 I have frequent headaches (not just hangovers!).			
9 My vision is blurred for no reason.			

Possible feelings about stress, and reactions to causes of stress: only tick one *column for each factor listed below*	This is me!	This is a bit like me	This isn't me at all
10 My neck and shoulders ache continuously.			
11 I frequently have skin rashes.			
12 My resistance to infection seems very low.			
13 I know I am far too irritable.			
14 I am smoking a lot.			
15 I could be drinking too much alcohol.			
16 I just don't seem to be able to concentrate.			
17 I often get strung up by everyday routine situations.			
18 I simply haven't got time for everything.			
19 There's too much change going on around me.			
20 I really don't think I'm up to this final year!			
21 There's just too much going on in my life in general just now, let alone it being my final year!			
22 It's not me, it's all those other people who stress me!			
Column totals			
Grand stress total			

Working out your stress score

Please follow these instructions carefully, one at a time.

1 For every entry you made in the 'This is me!' column, write in three stress points.

2 Add up your scores for the 'This is me!' column.

3 Check your addition really carefully.

4 For every entry in the 'This is a bit like me' column, write in one stress point.

5 Add up your scores for the 'This is a bit like me' column.

6 Check your addition again – it should be easier this time, all 'ones'.

7 For every entry you made in the 'This isn't me at all' column write in zero stress points.

8 Add up your scores for the 'This isn't like me at all' column.

9 If your total for the 'This isn't like me at all' column isn't zero, please seek help immediately.

10 Add up your grand total, and write it in the box at the foot of the table.

11 Finally, write your score on a blank sheet of paper, and have this ready for the analysis below.

Analysis

- If your grand stress total score was over 66, seek help immediately from someone who's better at arithmetic than you are – 66 was the maximum possible score.
- If you think your score is on the high side, look further into the rest of this chapter, and think about whether you're really *feeling* stressed, and decide, calmly and objectively, whether it could be worth you doing something about it yourself, or seeking help from those who are qualified to help sort out your reactions to stress – counsellors medical staff, etc.
- If your grand stress total score was exactly zero, I don't believe you, or you're abnormally unstressed, or you're a mechanical being.
- If the score on your sheet of paper is between 1 and 66, *and* you're not worried about it being too high, draw a ring round your score, then tear the sheet of paper up into quite small pieces. Try to derive considerable pleasure from doing this.
- If you really enjoyed that exercise, try it out on a friend, and compare your scores, then get your friend to tear up his or her sheet too.

So what can we do about stress?

You'll have gathered by now, if you completed the task, that I was pulling your leg somewhat! Listed in the table were indeed many of the most common symptoms associated with stress. Most of these symptoms are also commonly associated with life in general. If you have too many of these symptoms at once, you are probably not feeling at your best, and may well need to consider doing something about some of the symptoms, or having a rest, or enjoying yourself a little more, and so on.

Stress is normal. Too much stress is bad for us. Too little stress is bad for us. Some researchers into stress talk about two types: 'negative' stress, which they call 'distress', which can damage our work, and 'positive' stress, which they call 'eustress' – another word for 'pressure' – which makes us work better. It's worth looking at what actually happens in most of the situations we think of as stressful.

The immediate effect of stress on our bodies is that we prepare our resources to give us speed and strength. That's how we evolved. We needed strength and speed in the Stone Age when a larger animal wanted to eat us! Our bodies still respond to a situation of stress – be it just a red traffic light when running late – as though it were a rapidly approaching sabre-toothed tiger. We may have become more sophisticated and developed since the Stone Age, but our physical bodies have not changed their responses to stimuli very much. Our responses to stress are still those that came about from millions of years of evolution, and are designed to cope with dangers that are long gone from our lives. In most circumstances, the causes of stress are in fact less of a problem than are *our* responses to stress. We did not evolve to fight that sabre-toothed tiger 20 times each day – one in a month would have been enough to cope with. We need to become better-able to manage our *responses* to stress, rather than merely try to manage the *causes* of it.

Here's a summary of our immediate physical responses to stress:

- our brains adjust so as to feel pain less, so that thinking and memory can improve – good news so far;
- the pupils of our eyes dilate to give us better vision;
- our lungs take in more oxygen;
- our livers work harder to convert carbohydrates (stored as glycogen) into glucose, which provides us with more energy to fight or run;
- our hearts work harder to turn the extra oxygen and glucose into power – pulse rate and blood pressure both rise;
- our adrenal glands secrete adrenalin – the 'fight or flight' hormone;
- our digestion more or less halts, as the body diverts energy to our muscles;
- our body hair stands on end to make us look bigger and more dangerous to predators!

There are delayed responses too. These are much more serious if we are repeatedly stressed. The human body was not built to handle prolonged stress. The liver starts to convert fat to usable fuel. Most stress situations in modern life don't actually demand so much fuel, so the fats become re-stored near the liver – not the best place to build up a surplus of fat. At the same time the immune system reduces its efficiency, so as to release more energy to fight or run, and thus our infection-fighting mechanisms are diminished. The brain cortex secretes cortisol, which regulates our metabolism, but too much of this is poisonous to our brain cells, and can end up damaging cognitive ability, leading to fatigue, anger or depression. The decrease in blood flow in our intestines leaves them more vulnerable to ulcers. Increased blood pressure and heart rate damage the elasticity of our blood vessels.

The real problem is when we generate our natural responses to stress too often, in situations where we can't actually use all that extra strength and energy to fight off that predator!

Managing our responses to stress

It is widely accepted that what we call 'stress' is caused by an imbalance between *demands* on us (environmental pressures, if you like) and our *capacity* to meet these demands. If we feel we've got too many things to do, *and* not enough time to do them in, we feel stressed. Much more important (and much more in our own control than people tend to believe) is our *response* to stress. There is a great deal we can do to take control of our response to stress. Sometimes there's not much we can do about some of the causes of stress ('stressors'). If other people are the stressors, there may be nothing at all we can do about them. But if it's other people, it's not actually our problem. We can indeed do things about stressors which *are* our problem, and that's all we can do. We can minimize the effects (and symptoms) of many of our stressors.

Some stress tips

Your final year is a busy time of your life. It is a time when many things around you are changing quite rapidly. Change of any kind is recognized as a stressor, even when it's pleasant change. The list of tips below offers you some tried and tested advice for taking on the responsibility for watching out for your own stress symptoms, and minimizing the effects which stress has on you, your work, and the people around you. Pick the ones that will work best for you, and try them out.

- **Get better at recognizing the physical signs of stress.** These include the raised heart rate and blood pressure already mentioned above, along with increased sweating, headaches, dizziness, blurred vision, aching neck and shoulders, skin rashes, and lowered resistance to infection – many of which I included in the task on stress. When people are aware that such symptoms may be caused by stress, it helps them to look at their approaches to work to see if the causes of such symptoms may arise from stress.

- **Get better at recognizing the behavioural effects of stress.** These include increased anxiety, irritability, increased consumption of tobacco or alcohol, sleep disturbance, lack of concentration, and inability to deal calmly and efficiently with everyday tasks and situations.
- **Increase your awareness of how your own body reacts to stress.** Responses to stress happen in three distinct stages. 'The alarm reaction stage' causes defences to be set up and an increased release of adrenalin. 'The resistance stage' is when the body will resist the stressor, or adapt to the stress conditions. 'The exhaustion stage' results when attempts by the body to adapt have failed, and the body succumbs to the effects of stress. One of the purposes of this part of the book is to help you avoid being overcome by stress – you *can* avoid it!
- **Regard stress as temporary.** We evolved to deal with temporary stress, and our responses are designed to cope with this. If we allow ourselves to take the attitude that stress is permanent, we are heading for something we're *not* designed to cope with! For example, it's better to say to yourself 'I'm tired today' (temporary implications), than to say 'I'm washed up!' (permanent implications). Taking this argument further, it's better to say to yourself 'I have a bad habit at present' than 'I'm a bad person'.
- **Don't ignore stress.** There are no prizes for struggling to the point of collapse: indeed, this is the last thing you should be doing in your final year. As the symptoms of stress become apparent to you, try to identify the causes of your stress and do something about your responses to them. See below for a wide range of things you can do.
- **Get over the myths surrounding stress.** Research has shown that stress should not be regarded as the same as nervous tension, and is not always a negative response. Some people do indeed survive well and thrive on a lot of stress – at least for a limited period. In an education setting, such as your final year, which *is* a limited period, it is more important to manage stress than to try to eliminate it.
- **Look to the environmental causes of stress.** These include working or living under extremes of temperature, excessive noise, unsuitable lighting, poor ventilation or air quality, poorly laid-out work areas, and even the presence of vibration. If there is something like this affecting you, see what you can do about it. Most of these problems can be got round. Stronger light bulb? Extra jumper? Open a window? Tidy up?
- **Look to the social causes of stress.** These can include insufficient social contact, sexual harassment, racial discrimination, ageism,

inappropriate management approaches, unhealthy levels of competition, and conflict between colleagues. Some of these are very serious, even illegal. Your final year, however, is not the best time to seek justice or resolution if you're affected by stressors like these. Try to back away from being affected by them, for the present.

- **Look to the organizational causes of stress.** In the wider world outside university these include inappropriately heavy workloads, ineffective communication, excessive supervision or inadequate supervision, lack of relevant training provision, undue concern about promotion or re- ward systems, and unsatisfactory role perceptions. Once identified, all of these causes can be remedied in an organization. You might still feel that in your final year you have an 'inappropriately heavy workload', but so has everyone else.

- **Cultivate the right to feel stress, and to talk about it.** Stress is at its worst when it is bottled up and unresolved. It should be regarded as perfectly natural for people's stress levels to vary in the normal course of their work. The same goes for your final year. When stress is some- thing that can be discussed, it is much more likely that the causes can be addressed.

- **Allow yourself to *feel* anger, but be careful how you *express* it.** It isn't surprising that people under stress often feel full of rage, which is often not specifically directed. People often become very frustrated when they feel powerless, so it may be worth taking stock of what is and what is not within your control. Anger, once generated, can be released in many directions, and the most harmful of these is inwards. All the same, it is unwise as well as unprofessional to vent your rage on others, especially innocent bystanders who are caught in the crossfire. Find ways to let off steam that are not destructive to yourself and others.

- **Write it out of your system.** Some people find it very helpful to write about the issues that stress them and make them angry. This can take the form of a diary in which you record your feelings and analyse the situation, or letters you would like to send to the people who are causing you stress, or other forms of writing to take your mind off the current situation. You're in an excellent position to write it out of your system – throw yourself into the writing you *need* to do anyway: summaries to aid your revision, improving your CV, writing to friends, and so on.

- **Have some fun.** Look for ways in which you can de-stress yourself by doing things that make you happy. A little hedonism goes a long way. Think about the things that give you pleasure like cooking, reading for pleasure, going to concerts or having a day of total sloth. Regard these as part of a programme of active stress management rather than as a guilt-inducing interference with your work. You deserve some time for yourself, not least during the busiest times of your final year, and you shouldn't regard it as a luxury.

- **Don't be afraid to go to the doctor.** The worst excesses of stress can be helped by short-term medication and medical intervention of some kind. People are often unwilling to resort to a visit to their GP for stress-related matters when they wouldn't hesitate to seek help for a physical ailment. Don't let such feelings get in the way of seeking the kind of support you need.

- **Try not to worry about not sleeping.** Sleep disturbance is one of the most common features of stress and worrying about it makes it worse. Try to ensure that you are warm and comfortable at bedtime, avoid working for at least an hour before you retire and use music or reading to help get you into a relaxed state. If sleep doesn't come, try to use the rest period to recoup some energy and try not to go over and over in your mind what is troubling you. Taking exercise and cutting down on your caffeine intake can help.

- **Use relaxation techniques.** There are innumerable methods that can be used to help you unwind, including deep breathing, massage, aromatherapy and meditation. It might be worth your while to explore the techniques that sound most attractive to you and try to use them to help you cope with stress.

- **Take exercise.** Taking physical exercise at the end of a long stressful day may be the last thing you feel like doing, but lots of people find it helps them relax. Join a gym, take someone's dog for long walks, swim, take up golf, play a mean game of squash or just do aerobics at home to help your body to become as tired physically as your mind is mentally. Find out what kinds of exercise work best for you and try to use them as a bridge between your studying life and your own time. Try not to let your exercise requirement end up feeling like another kind of work you have to do!

- **Get a life outside university.** Family and friends still deserve your attention, even if you are very busy studying. We all need to learn to keep a sense of proportion in our lives. Try not to neglect hobbies and interests, even if you sleep through the film or nod off after the sweet course when having a meal out with friends. Let animals help you to remember how to be a human, too – borrow a pet for an evening!

- **Take a break.** Often our panics over time management are caused not so much by how much we have to do as by whether we feel we have sufficient time to do it in. Try to take a real break from time to time, so as to help you get your workload into proportion. An occasional mini-holiday or a whole weekend without final-year work can make you better able to cope with the onslaught on your return.

- **Overcome powerlessness with action.** When you are stressed out, it is often because you feel totally powerless in the situation. It can be useful to look at the areas you do have some control over and try to do something about them, however minor. This may not change the overall picture very much, but will probably make you feel better.
- **Talk about your problems.** Actually voicing what is stressing you to a fellow student, a lecturer, the person you are closest to or even someone's cat can sometimes improve the situation. Bottling it all up through some misplaced sense of fortitude can be dangerous.
- **Try counselling.** All colleges have someone to whom students (and staff) can turn for trained counselling in times of great stress. Yes, your lecturers get stressed too! Otherwise you could look elsewhere: consult your GP or look in the phone book under 'therapists' or 'alternative medicine' to find someone who can guide and support you through the worst patches. This is often more productive than piling all your stress onto your closest friends, who usually have problems of their own!
- **Try not to personalize a stress situation.** It is easy to fall into the trap of seeing all your stress as being caused by an individual or group of people who have it in for you. Of course this may be the case, but usually high stress situations are caused by cock-up rather than conspiracy!
- **Avoid compounding the problem.** If things overall are pretty stressful in your final year, try to avoid making important life changes at the same time. This is not the best time to decide to go entirely vegetarian, give up smoking or move house.
- **Audit your intake of stimulants.** For those whose culture allows alcohol, a little can be felt to be a wonderful relaxant, but excessive intakes can be problematic. It's natural to drink a lot of beverages containing caffeine when trying to get through a lot of work, but it can interfere with your metabolism and sleep patterns. Eating rich food too late at night and smoking too much can also get in the way of being calm. Moderation is boring but is a good policy for those under stress.
- **Try to adopt a long-term perspective.** It can be really hard to project into the future and to review current stress as part of a much larger pattern, but if you can do it, it helps. Much of what seems really important now will pale into insignificance in a few weeks, months or years time. Next year won't be your final year. There will still be other causes of stress for you to manage. Get good at managing stress now.
- **A problem shared can be a problem doubled!** Stressed people meeting in groups can reinforce each other's stress levels by constantly rehearsing their shared problems. Talking to people is good, however. Find some other people to talk to, about *other* things.

Final words about stress

You *need* to be sufficiently stressed in your final year, to show your full potential, and to grow into a person who is better-equipped to manage the stresses of the future, and to help others to manage their stress levels. Keep stress under *your* control. Monitor it. Don't worry about it. Work on being in control of your responses to it. Also work on avoiding those stressful situations which are not necessary for you. You don't need to go searching for a sabre-toothed tiger! Don't agonize over the 'if only . . .' agenda. Get on with your final year, and get a life at the same time – but not for too much of the time.

 Personal action plan

This could be a good time for you to write yourself a few resolutions. Some of these may be based upon things mentioned in this chapter. Take a few minutes to capture your thoughts by jotting them down, and plan how you could save yourself many hours later.

What sort of degree am I really aiming for?

One studying habit I'm going to change:

One thing I'm going to do to keep my final year in tune with the rest of my world:

One enemy I've identified:

Two ways I'm going to increase my learning pay-off:

Two time management tactics I'm going to try out:

How I plan to continue working well even in 'captivity' – such as during lectures, and so on:

One adjustment in attitude to lecturers I'm going to try out:

Two pieces of evidence I'm going to gather for use towards my future career:

What I've concluded about my responses to stress:

Two tactics I'm going to try out to manage my stress levels:

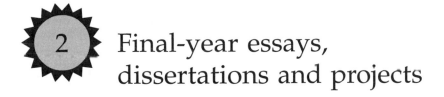

2 Final-year essays, dissertations and projects

▶ Final-year tasks seem much bigger!

Why do the assignments you're set in your final year get bigger? There are several factors involved, including:

- You're likely to be in a smaller group than you were in previous years, and your lecturers and tutors have more time and energy to handle the results of you doing longer, more complex assignments.
- The subjects are getting harder, or you're going into a narrow range of subject matter in much greater depth than you did in previous years. Longer assignments are required to allow you to demonstrate that you're digging deeper.
- Your assessors are looking for evidence of a higher level of development than they may have been seeking in previous years. Depending on your subject area, your assessors are likely to be looking for evidence of:
  - critical analysis;
  - problem solving;
  - power of argument;
  - creativity;
  - originality;
  - your ability to set about some primary research;
  - your ability to make use of secondary research (what's already been done);
  - skills at learning independently;
  - ability to take up an idea and run with it;
  - ability to see the wood for the trees;
  - ability to find, and cite properly, relevant information from the published literature;
  - ability to track down relevant information from the Internet, and find out how authentic it is;

- mastery rather than just competence;
- high-level written communication;
- good oral communication (being able to handle being put on the spot).
- At least some (perhaps all) of the tasks you're set in your final year will count towards the level of your final qualification, so high quality, tangible evidence is sought regarding the level of your own development that you can demonstrate.

You may well be required to undertake a research project in your final year, and to write up your results and conclusions in an extended project report, or a dissertation, which shows a combination of some or all of the abilities in the list above.

What are the dangers associated with large tasks?

Here are some of the main ones:

- Putting off for too long the dreaded moment of getting started.
- Not looking carefully enough at the information that is given to you (or is lodged in course documentation and/or student handbooks) about the assessment *criteria* that will be applied to the products of your thinking, such as your essays, dissertation or research report, and so on.
- Spending too much time and energy on the large tasks, and leaving undone important smaller tasks which still count towards your final qualification.
- Spending too long getting the big tasks well under way, and leaving yourself too little time for editing, polishing, second thoughts, further development of your ideas, and so on.
- Becoming tired and stale, and not delivering the quality of evidence that you could otherwise have achieved.
- Not getting started early enough on the *other* important big tasks of your final year, such as getting your act together to apply successfully for jobs, or for research opportunities.

The real enemies are not getting started soon enough, and getting behind schedule in general. If you're working against tight deadlines, and something else delays you, or some part of your task takes longer than you'd planned, everything seems desperate. When you're under pressure, your brain does not function as well as it can when you've not got such additional worries.

How do you eat an elephant?

The short answer is 'one bite at a time'. Any large task can be managed more successfully if you apply the following approaches to it:

- Get started on it right away.
- Think about it often, but always with a pen in your hand (or at your computer). How often have you thought of a brilliant idea, only to have forgotten it again by the time you're ready to put it into action? Jot your ideas down straightaway – rough notes will do, such as Post-its in your pocket.
- Do a little of it regularly, rather than a lot at once.
- Break the back of it quite early, leaving yourself plenty of opportunity to improve and develop it.
- Keep planning and re-planning, to make sure that you don't drift off into unnecessary diversions.
- Keep looking back at what you've done, editing and improving it all the time.
- Get well ahead of schedule, so that you've got plenty of opportunity to spend a little time, regularly, polishing your evidence.
- Use all the *other* things you need to do concurrently as 'welcome breaks' from the big tasks, rather than 'unwelcome interruptions'.

Getting ahead with the large tasks also means that you'll feel better about yourself. You're more confident when you're not struggling against deadlines. Life is better!

▶ Getting the level right for your final year

This is a tricky one! What is the 'right' level? Who can tell you about it? How can you tell when you're getting there? Final-year work is obviously supposed to be at a higher level than your previous work. You're ex-pected to have matured and developed intellectually during your time at university. In some disciplines there are clear clues regarding the level that is expected of you. For example, in maths or most science and engin-eering areas, you can tell a lot about the level from the kinds of problem you're asked to tackle.

In other subjects, such as humanities, business and so on, it can be harder to work out what's expected of you. You will then need to use your wits, and set about systematically *finding out* about the level required. What tactics can you select from? Here are a few:

- Make really good use of each and every element of feedback on your own work that you get from tutors or lecturers. Listen carefully to what they say to you, then go away and jot down very short notes on *all* the feedback, positive and negative, so that you don't forget any-thing useful.
- Look for clues from lecturers in lectures, and particularly in tutorials or small-group work. Again, jot down the clues. However sensible a piece

of advice seems at the time, it's human nature to forget most of it unless we capture it somehow.

- Get your hands on the assessment criteria for big final-year tasks. These criteria are usually made explicit in course documentation, and are often explained further in student handbooks. Your lecturers and assessors may well assume that because you've been given such information, you have automatically studied it carefully. External examiners' roles include checking very carefully that these assessment criteria have been applied fairly and consistently. The more you tune in to the criteria, the better your evidence will reflect them.
- Keep an eye on your fellow students' work levels. Work with them, talk with them, look at their work, show them yours. Spend more time with people who seem to be getting the level right. Also spend some time explaining things that you've mastered to other students who haven't yet mastered them – this is good for your own learning and particularly good for developing your powers of demonstrating what you know and expressing it well.
- Work out, if necessary by a little trial and error, what your lecturers' expectations are regarding those higher-level skills such as originality, creativity, lateral thinking, critical argument, and so on.
- Get hold of any past exam papers, or past assignment briefings for your course. Don't just hoard these. Look at them every week. They're your targets. They show you the standards you're aiming towards. Don't let them frighten you – you're not expected to be able to answer your final exam questions in Week 1! But still keep looking at them. When the questions are planted in your mind, you'll be much more receptive to the *answers* as they unfold in your lectures, tutorials and reading.

Final-year writing style?

You might think that by now you know how to write. You'll already know a lot about the expected style in your discipline. This varies a lot from one discipline to another. However, the most frequent complaint of assessors is that too many candidates simply don't know how to write well! Whether you're writing essays, reports or a dissertation, you still need to write well. Whether you're using a word processor for some assessed coursework, or sitting with a pen in an exam room, it's the words that you write (or type) which are measured. Essays in exams are very different from coursework essays, and need to be tackled in quite different ways, but a common key factor remains writing style. Assessors can't measure what's inside your head, other than through the words you use to express your knowledge and ability. If your writing style is well-developed, you'll always get quite a lot more credit than you would have done, on the same knowledge base, using a poorer style.

Is it too late to improve my writing style?

It's never too late. There's nothing magical about good writing. No major operation is needed on your brain to turn you into a better writer. As far back as 1818, William Cobbett declared that 'the *only* use of words is to *cause our meaning to be clearly understood'*. What about grammar, spelling and punctuation? You'll always lose some credit if your use of language is erratic or irregular. If you use 'it's' (short for 'it is') when you mean 'its' (belonging to it), even if no marks are deducted, you've lost some headway in the 'benefit of the doubt' stakes. If you use 'principal' when you mean 'principle' you'll offend some assessors. (The principal benefit to be gained from the principles of good use of language is a higher grade for your writing!)

What about punctuation? There are some rules here, and they are quite easy to learn though they are sometimes interpreted rather flexibly. For example, some argue that double quotes "..." should only be used for reported speech, and single quotes for everything else. However, many would argue that double quotes can be used *within* single quotes (or vice-versa) when a quotation is being made within another quotation. For example, earlier in this chapter I mentioned: 'As for back as 1818, William Cobbett declared that "the only use of words is to cause our meaning to be clearly understood" '. Using single quotes for 'emphasis' is frowned upon by many assessors. It is better to *underline* for emphasis, or use *italics* or **bold** if you're word-processing. Don't use too many commas in one sentence. Too many commas cause confusion. Use a comma when, if you were reading the sentence out loud, you would pause slightly. Use a semicolon if you're separating two parts of a long sentence; in practice the semicolon is the most misused punctuation element. Semicolons can also be used after items in a list of bullet points. Colons are also often misused. They are properly used:

- before explanations, for example, 'We have had to abandon our day trip: the car wouldn't start';
- before a list, for example, 'The main points are as follows:';
- to introduce quotations;
- in titles, to separate a main heading from a sub-heading;
- in figure/table titles, for example 'Figure 4: Map of . . .'.

How best can you improve your grammar, spelling and punctuation? There are many books in the library. Spell checkers on your computer may be able to help (but won't sort out your principles from your principal).

The best way to find out about your black spots is to ask someone to tell you about them. Give a friend (or a friendly tutor) a piece of your writing, and ask 'just tell me about the grammar in this'. Try two or three people with the same piece – you'll get some different replies, but the common ground is worth looking at carefully.

But is that all there is to 'style'?

Of course not. It's just that however good your style becomes, you'll still not make your best impact if the words are wrong. Some important aspects of good style for extended pieces of final-year work include:

- Making the beginning explain *why*. The start of any extended piece of writing needs to give the purpose of all of the rest of it. First impressions are important.
- Making the middle hang together, and *not* losing your reader.
- Ending well: last impressions are really important when the grade or mark you will be awarded is the next decision for your assessor.

But that's still not all. In fact, the points listed above are more to do with *structure* than style. Style is additionally about *how* you say what you're saying. It's about the words, phrases and expressions which you choose and use. It's about impact. Long academic sentences with several clauses and sub-clauses in them don't always have more impact than well-placed, short statements. Style is what makes *your* writing different from other people's. It's the style that is the give-away when an assessor notices an inserted paragraph which was obviously written by someone else.

However, there is still nothing magical about style. It boils down to a set of skills which can be learned. To develop your style:

- play with it in your informal writing;
- test it out on other people – all feedback is useful;
- look at other people's style when you read books and articles;
- look at how journalists get messages across in newspapers;
- research the styles that are used most widely in your own discipline areas;
- research the styles that are preferred by the people who will be assessing yours!

In very broad terms, for example, in humanities subjects, social sciences and literature studies, eloquence of written style features high in the assessment stakes. These disciplines are also those where assessors are most likely to be seeking quite highly individual styles. In literature, the styles adopted by famous writers are analysed in depth, and you may do well to find out which of the facets of their styles would be worth adopting or adapting into your own style.

In science and engineering there is broader consensus on style, and the emphasis may be more on the factual content of your writing, and the logic of the order in which you present your findings, ideas, comparisons and so on. It is also traditional to use phrases such as 'it was observed that', rather than 'I noticed that' – in other words, the tone tends to be third-person passive. Many people now see the value of a less formal approach, but if your assessors are among those who expect you to write in a formal, authoritative manner, you should humour them.

In business and management disciplines, the emphasis in some topic areas may be more on authoritative reasoning and decision-making. Here too an eloquence of style distinguishes the best candidates from the rest. Look at it the other way: if you practise and deliver eloquence of style, you may be judged to be writing well. However, sophistication of style is fine, so long as your meaning gets across clearly and quickly. Many are the candidates who have sacrificed the meaning of an important thought by writing out a sentence in an exam answer, such that the sentence was too long for its meaning to be gathered correctly.

In maths, there's still a 'style' to how you go about solving problems. You'll get more credit for getting the right answer by the most sensible, direct method, and for making it clear exactly how you got there. Assessors and examiners lose patience with long-way-round attempts, even when they are successful. After all, if you know how to solve a problem directly and quickly, it shows that you understand more about it than if you play around with indirect approaches. Besides, if you take long ways round in exams, you're penalizing yourself by reducing the time you've got left for all the other questions.

▶ Making sure that big important jobs don't shield you from small important jobs!

Work expands, it is said, to fill the available time. This is only true, however, if your time management (and task management) are both in need of an overhaul. It is also said, as I mentioned earlier in this book, that stress is not so much about having too much to do, as about having the feeling that you have too little time to do it in. Overhaul your task management strategy now, and spare yourself from a lot of potential stress.

During your final year, you'll have several big important jobs, which may include:

- getting ready for your final exams;
- getting ready for the possibility of an oral exam (viva) after your written exams;

- putting together a dissertation or major report;
- preparing, perhaps, a presentation based upon your dissertation, which may count significantly towards your final degree;
- building yourself a good CV;
- accumulating evidence of your strengths and talents, perhaps in the form of a portfolio of your work, to show to potential employers;
- lining up your future.

There will also be all the small important jobs, most of which you'll be well-used to handling, for example:

- doing smaller coursework elements, such as essays or practical reports, or preparing to give a seminar, and so on;
- getting to grips with the continuing content of your lectures, tutorials and seminars;
- trying to get yourself significantly *ahead* of the delivery of your course, so that during lectures, tutorials and seminars you're doing much more learning than if you were thinking about the content for the first time;
- managing the rest of your life!

Getting the balance wrong between the big jobs and the small jobs is dangerous either way. One of the biggest hazards is spending too much time on the *new* agendas associated with the big important jobs, and not leaving yourself enough leeway to be strategic and systematic about the small important jobs. Some students find the reverse hazard, and spend so much time doing the familiar, small important jobs that they don't get started sufficiently early on the big important ones. In this situation, the time management and task management ideas mentioned in Chapter 1 come into their own, for example:

- get *one* important small job right out of the way before turning your attention to one of the big jobs;
- tackle the big jobs a bit at a time, and set yourself a manageable chunk of *one* of these to do (for example) in the next hour;
- keep coming back to the big jobs, regularly, so that you can allow your subconscious mind to continue thinking about them while you're doing other things, and reap the benefits of that subconscious thought each time you pick up the threads of the big jobs once more;
- spend each working day doing bits of *more* than one of the big jobs (as well as one or two smaller ones), so that you don't get sucked into spending too much time on any one of them;
- regard switching onto a different task as being good for your brain – a change being as good as a rest – rather than feeling that you're escaping from one task to another.

▶ Drafting and redrafting your work quickly and efficiently

If you're already well used to working with word-processing software, you'll already know how much easier it is to edit and polish your written work on a word processor than with pen and paper. You will also have found, however, that you need to see your work on paper sometimes, rather than on a screen. It's hard to get the feel of a long piece of writing just by looking at a screen. It's easier to flick through the pages of a printout, than to scroll up and down an on-screen document.

Working with a computer, you can continue to adjust the order in which you present ideas by cutting and pasting sentences, paragraphs or whole sections of an essay, report or dissertation. Here are some suggestions for maximizing the benefits you reap while drafting and redrafting your work (and this includes your CV).

- **Plan before you even start serious writing.** Sketch out an 'egg diagram' or mind-map about whatever you're going to be working on. Do this in a free-flowing brainstorming mode, using keywords and questions to alert you to the research you will do on your way towards your target. For example, if you were going to start to write an essay (or even a dissertation) on 'Public transport and economic policy' your first plan could look like the egg diagram shown in Figure 2.1.

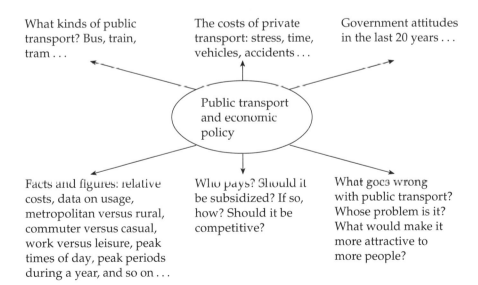

What kinds of public transport? Bus, train, tram . . .

The costs of private transport: stress, time, vehicles, accidents . . .

Government attitudes in the last 20 years . . .

Public transport and economic policy

Facts and figures: relative costs, data on usage, metropolitan versus rural, commuter versus casual, work versus leisure, peak times of day, peak periods during a year, and so on . . .

Who pays? Should it be subsidized? If so, how? Should it be competitive?

What goes wrong with public transport? Whose problem is it? What would make it more attractive to more people?

Figure 2.1 Egg diagram for essay 'Public transport and economic policy'

- **Don't start writing whole sentences yet!** When you've spent a few minutes jotting down everything you can think of in terms of ideas and questions, start putting numbers beside each idea, in the order which seems most sensible for knitting the ideas together into a coherent whole.
- **Still don't write whole sentences yet!** Keep returning to your plan. Stick it to a wall so you can keep it in sight when writing. Add new ideas to it as soon as you think of them. Don't worry yet about the order, you can write further numbers to slip ideas 6a and 6b between your existing ideas 6 and 7, and so on.
- **Set your sights on getting a good first draft ready at a very early stage.** The sooner you've got a first draft, the more chance you have to make your final draft a good one. Aim to have a first draft ready within a tenth of your total timescale. This could mean quite soon!
- **Now start fleshing out your ideas.** Each idea may become a paragraph (or a subheading) in your first draft. If you're working with pen and paper, it can be useful to develop each idea on a fresh sheet of paper. This means you can continue to shuffle your ideas on a desk, table or the floor, and continue to work at getting the most sensible order in which to link them together. If you're working on a word processor, you can rearrange the ideas at any time, but it's sometimes better to have them on bits of paper at this stage so you can keep an eye on the big picture of your developing piece as you work towards the detail. Remember that a paragraph should be rather like a single thought. All of it should hang together. It shouldn't contain too many thoughts.
- **After you've drafted out a paragraph, come back to its meaning and think more deeply about how you're going to start it.** The first sentence in the paragraph needs to say why the rest of it is there, and why it's important. In addition, that first sentence needs to have impact. It needs to be interesting. It needs to be *you* speaking.
- *Don't* **worry too much about the introduction at this stage.** The *best* time to write your introduction is when you've just about finished the piece. This applies to everything from an essay to a dissertation to a whole book! Only when you've finished are you really in a position to write a good, solid introduction, which will be lived up to by the rest of your piece.
- *Do* **start thinking about how you want to end your piece.** Work out what are your important conclusions, decisions or recommendations. Keep tabs on these, so that you can, in due course, bring them together into a solid, tight 'end' section.
- **Keep stopping and putting your work away!** Then look at it again, and read what's *actually* there, as if from fresh. You'll be surprised at how often, after a day or two, you can see better ways of saying what you wrote. You may also have new ideas to work into what's already there. Keep redrafting.

- **Get as much feedback as you can on what you're writing**. Show other people, and ask them to tell you what they think. Get other people to scribble comments and reactions onto a copy of the bits and pieces you're stitching together. Obviously, you may not want to reveal all of your ideas to a fellow student who may be tackling exactly the same task as you are, but there are plenty of other people around you, some of whom may have really useful ideas.
- **Start putting together your first full draft**. Keep to length. If a word limit has been given, work as closely as you reasonably can to it. If your work is far too long, your assessors could get bored with it! If it's far too short, you're not likely to get good marks for it either.
- **Continue to edit and adjust**. Improve your piece on the basis of feedback. Improve it with your own second thoughts, third thoughts and fourth thoughts.

It is said by many writers that a major piece of writing is never finished – it is merely abandoned at the least damaging point! Don't redraft *too* much. When you've done *most* of what you can do with your piece of work, it's probably time to move on to something else – chase after some *different* marks.

▶ Watch out for accusations of plagiarism and cheating!

If you're accused of these things during your final year you're in big trouble! Even if you're entirely innocent, the stigma may stick. It's fairly obvious what 'cheating' usually means: for example using someone else's work as your own, or carrying into an exam room crib notes or other prohibited sources of information.

The boundaries between *properly* referring to other people's work and plagiarism are much less well defined. In your final year, one of the major expectations that your lecturers and examiners have is that you will display your ability to find things in the literature, and to compare and contrast other people's ideas, theories, models, findings, analyses, deductions, speculations, proposals and so on. You may also be expected to exercise your critical judgement on other people's published work. You are quite likely to be expected not only to search established textbooks and respected journals, but also to look for other people's views as published on the Internet, in which case you are likely to be required to make judgements about how authentic and credible are the electronic sources of information you find. (It's easier to judge the credibility and authenticity of an article published in a respected journal in your field, as the journal's referees have already verified and validated it before publication.)

You will often be asked to show where *your* views fit in with other people's work. You will very often be expected to quote extracts from other people's published work verbatim in your own essays, your dissertation, in reports and so on. In open-book exams, if you have them, you could be expected to make similar verbatim quotes from the resources in front of you in the exam room, so that you can make it clear *exactly* what you're then going to discuss yourself.

All this is fine, and safe, as long as you *acknowledge very clearly* which of the words and ideas that you write belong to other people. Especially when quoting verbatim, it is quite essential that you say that that is what you're doing, and identify your source *exactly*, and in the format which your lecturers and assessors are expecting from you.

Getting your referencing right is more important than you may think. You could be thinking that those of your lecturers who are fussy about this are being unreasonable, but they aren't! When you yourself come to send your research writing off to journals, or your books to publishers, you'll find that editors and copy-editors are *really* pernickety about references. Even before that, assessors of your dissertation will look hard at your bibliography, not just to see that you've referred to important work that they know about (including their own!), but also to see whether you're careful with your referencing. A well-referenced piece of work is usually taken as a sign that it's a *good* piece of work, so you can actually expect to end up getting some extra marks just for good referencing (though this might not appear among the published assessment criteria). If you've forgotten how to cite work properly, or have never quite got the hang of it, read on.

A reminder about referencing protocols

The most accepted system for referencing is the 'Harvard' system, illustrated below. There are some differences between referencing journal articles, and books. There are also differences in how to cite the reference in your own text, depending upon the context, and whether you're quoting directly or not, or just putting the author's views into your own words. So that I've got no one to blame but myself if I get things wrong, I'll refer to some other things I've written or co-written in the examples below!

Journal articles

In the text of your article, the citation of one of my journal articles could take one of these three forms:

> Race (1998) suggests that transferable skills are now being regarded as being of increased importance in higher education.

Or:

It has been argued that transferable skills should be regarded as being of increased importance in higher education (Race 1998).

Or:

The view has been expressed that transferable skills 'have for too long been treated as the poor relations of subject-specific knowledge and skills. It is increasingly recognised that they are every bit as important' (Race 1998: 268).

Note that the page number from which the quotation is taken (268) is expected when you make a direct quotation, but is not necessary if you're just referring to the general idea.

In the references at the end of your piece, the Harvard way of citing this article is as follows:

Race, P. (1998) An education and training toolkit for the new millennium? *Innovations in Education and Training International*, **35**(3): 262–71.

The '35' refers to the volume number, the '3' in this case means it is the third part of that volume, and the '262–71' are the page numbers of the article.

Books

It has been suggested that in an organization, it is just as important that employees have a sense of well-being, as that they are in fact healthy (Day *et al.* 1999).

Or:

It is proposed that 'Wellness is as much about how people *feel* as about how they *are*' (Day *et al.* 1999: 66).

Note that '*et al.*' is used when there are three or more authors, and that you have to go to the full reference, listed in the Bibliography or References section, to find out who '*et al.*' actually are. The full reference to this book would appear as follows:

Day, A., Peters, J. and Race, P. (1999) *500 Tips for Developing a Learning Organization*. London: Kogan Page.

When there are *two* co-authors, it's usual to put both names in the text, for example:

A range of different methods of gathering and analysing feedback from students is explored by Race and Brown (1998).

Note that for a book, the *title* is put in italics (or underlined if you're doing it in handwriting), and for a journal article the *name of the journal* (not the article title) is put in italics (or underlined). Note that when quoting directly from a source, you should follow the original spelling style. For example, if the source spells 'sulfuric' rather than 'sulphuric', stick to the original spelling when quoting verbatim.

There are some variations on the main principles shown above: authors' forenames are quite often used instead of just initials, and some journals don't use a full stop (period if you're from North America) after initials. If a book or article is *edited* by author(s) rather than written by them, (ed.) or (eds) is placed after their names, and before the date of publication.

There are many good accounts of exactly how to use the Harvard system; if you need to do more than simply cite or quote from articles and books, you can find such a source in most research methodology books (for example, Denscombe 1998). Now look this up in the 'References and further reading' section at the end of this book and see whether I've referenced it correctly!

▶ Maximizing first (and last) impressions

Starting strongly

I've already hinted at the importance of first and last impressions. Imagine that *you* are assessing a pile of examples of the same sort of writing as you're doing. Imagine yourself with a pile of essays, or reports, or a roomful of dissertations! Imagine that you haven't actually got a great deal of time to spend assessing them and deciding the marks or grades that they deserve. You're going to want to find out straightaway how good (or bad) each of them is. That's where introductions are particularly important. You get no second chance to make a good first impression.

What do lecturers or tutors look for in a good introduction? Here are some of the questions in their minds as they read yours:

- Am I going to enjoy reading the rest of this?
- Is it stating the obvious, or leading me towards interesting ideas?
- Is it clear and unambiguous, or am I going to have to read each sentence three times before I find out what it really means?
- Is it showing that *this* candidate is going to really address the question or topic, and not get carried away on irrelevant tracks?
- Where is this piece going?
- Why has the author chosen this way to start it?
- Will the rest of the piece live up to the promise of the introduction?

- Is this going to be a good piece, an excellent one, a bad one, or a run-of-the-mill one?

Try to make each introduction you write address such questions. If you can lead your assessors into *expecting* that the piece they are just starting to assess is going to be a good one, they're more likely to be looking for the strengths which are to follow. If they already believe it's going to be a bad piece, they'll be looking for the weaknesses that they now expect! You can see now why something as important as your introduction needs to be done *last*, and done *well*.

Continuing coherently

Some questions in assessors' minds while they mark the main parts of your work include the following:

- Is this really answering the question, or addressing the brief as given?
- Did the candidate think of this, or is it adapted (or copied) from other people's work?
- Has the candidate made sensible use of the existing literature, and are all references properly listed at the end?
- Are the candidate's references to the literature well chosen and important, and not just the first ones that the candidate laid their hands on?
- Is the piece following on from what was promised by the introduction?
- Is it presented in a sensible, coherent order?
- Is each paragraph really a paragraph, addressing a single main idea?
- Am I enjoying reading this?
- Are there important things missing in this?
- Are there internal inconsistencies or contradictions in what the candidate says?

Remember that these questions (and many more like them) are in assessors' minds all the way through. How your piece addresses such questions profoundly influences how they give you marks!

Exemplary endings

Now what about the end? There's also no second chance to make a good *last* impression! How you end your piece will resonate in assessors' minds as they move from *reading* it to *deciding* how much it's worth. Within a minute or two of reaching the end of your work, they go into judgement mode. The best way to end a piece varies depending upon the nature of the question or topic, but some of the questions in assessors' minds now include:

- Has the candidate summarized the main conclusions reached in the piece?
- Has the candidate made decisions about things where decisions were required?
- Has the piece shown the sort of critical thinking I was looking for?
- Was this a first-class piece, or an upper-second class piece, or something else?
- Is the candidate's own view given where appropriate, rather than just other people's?
- Was the piece well researched, including references to the sources which I would have expected, and some more as well?

Assessors will be making up their minds about marks or grades on the basis of questions such as those above, while still remembering your last paragraph or two, in particular. The better they feel about how you ended your piece, the more likely you are to get better grades.

 Personal action plan

This chapter may have got you thinking about several different aspects of the challenges of your final year. Jot down your own answers to the following questions, as a way of retaining some of your best thoughts.

What kinds of evidence of 'higher-level development' do you think *you* should work at hardest (or smartest) in your final-year written work?

What are *your* most significant danger areas when it comes to putting together an extended piece of written work? And how are you now intending to tackle these danger areas?

What are you going to do to check out your writing style?

What are the most important things *you* still need to find out about the assessment culture you're working in?

What is your best tactic for making sure that small important jobs get done alongside big important ones?

Jot down two typical small important tasks that you'll need to get done. (Then perhaps go and do one of them right away.)

Which of the ideas in the section on drafting and redrafting is going to be most useful to you?

Which point on referencing protocols is most important in the sort of writing you'll be doing in your final year?

What are you going to do to maximize first impressions when your work is assessed?

What are you going to do to get the most benefit from last impressions?

3 Spills, skills, frills and thrills in your final year

▶ First, the spills

Your final year can feel like a bumpy ride at times. There is always the possibility of some 'spills' on this journey. Even though they're just about all avoidable, there are so many possibilities that statistically you should expect one or two.

Task: what's the worst that could happen to you?

Get it out of your system now. Jot down in this box two or three things that are your worst nightmares about being in your final year. What scares you rigid?

Did any of the nightmares you jotted in the box include your death? Very unlikely. Final-year students tend to survive. Did they involve you in serious physical injury? The vast majority of final-year students end the year more or less intact. Was the sabre-toothed tiger real or imaginary? Imaginary ones are more scary! Was the worst that could happen to you actually something that could happen to someone else – a disaster that might befall a partner, friend, relative and so on? These things do happen, and can be worse than most nightmares, but most students still manage to get through their final year despite the traumas that can be caused by happenings to significant others.

Or were your nightmares a lot less tangible? Are you simply terrified about your final year and scared of not knowing exactly what you should be terrified of? Are you scared simply because you think it's *right* to be scared now? Are you terrified because other people seem to be so, and you feel there must be something wrong with you if you're not? Or are you worried now, because you're *not* actually worried, and think you should be? Or is it the magnitude of the whole thing – so much to do, in so many different directions, and all at once, and never enough time to do anything well enough, and so on? That's understandable, but unnecessary. Your final year is like a huge jigsaw, made up of thousands of pieces. You can only fit in one small piece at a time. You can't assemble the whole thing at once – you've only got two hands.

So what are the *real* spills?

Most of them are quite minor events compared to death, injury or the other main traumas of normal life. The spills you may meet in your final year can include things like:

- Finding out that you've got a last-chance deadline for a piece of coursework which counts towards your degree, that you've forgotten about amidst all sorts of other demands.
- Finding out quite late that there's a topic in one of your exams on which you need to spend more time than you have left.
- Needing to do something at quite short notice in your job-hunting activities when you've not budgeted any time for it.
- Needing to spend time on a relationship which is suffering because you're so busy.
- Events beyond your control cropping up outside your studying or job hunting, such as family illness, a dose of flu, a bad toothache, and so on – things which under normal circumstances you'd cope with well enough, but which can seem disastrous when your schedule is full already.
- Missing a connection on your way to an interview, and feeling desperate about the possibility (or certainty) of being seen to arrive late.

Spills like this can easily become distorted out of their normal perspective when you feel that you've just not got enough time or energy to cope with a single thing more. At times like this, it's best to adopt the approach that there's only so much you can do, and do only that much.

In particular, it's just not a good idea to get into the blame culture. You don't do yourself any good by piling blame onto yourself about all the things you might have been able to do to avoid such spills. Tempting as it is to have some other people to blame instead, it doesn't actually solve anything to use up your energy redirecting the blame onto them, even when it's patently their fault. When people become stressed, it's very easy for them to blow quite minor incidents up out of all proportion, when the plain fact is that the time they spend doing this just adds to the stress. Try to head for win-win solutions to any problems with people, rather than try to win yourself and make them lose.

Regard problems as learning opportunities. Use the spills to help yourself, rather than take you down. Use them as learning experiences. Try to learn something useful about yourself from each thing that goes wrong. Try to identify ways that you can act in future to avoid each particular occurrence. This is, in fact, part of a much bigger picture – becoming more skilled, in all sorts of ways.

Turning setbacks into learning experiences: reflecting and collecting

You've probably had your fill of people telling you that everything unpleasant is a valuable learning experience! It does not seem to help at the time. Yet there's at least some truth in it. Some people believe that no real progress happens without at least some pain. Growing pains, they say.

The best way to capitalize on setbacks is to learn from them, but it's human nature to want to escape from them and put them far out of mind. However, if you make yourself an agenda to apply during, or after, an unwelcome 'learning experience', you may indeed find that it convinces you that it's worth investing in reflecting and collecting. Reflecting on what? Collecting what?

Here are some of the questions you could ask yourself about a setback:

- **Why did that happen?** What were the reasons for the setback? Which of these reasons could not have been avoided? Which of the reasons were such that you could have done something about them?
- **What exactly *was* the setback?** Which part of the complex chain of events was the core element of the setback?
- **Who, if anyone, was to blame?** Perhaps it was no one's fault, and was entirely unpredictable. Perhaps it was that rare occurrence, a genuine accident.
- **What courses of action did you have?** Did you choose the best one? Did it matter, in the long run, if you chose a slower road to recovery?
- **What did you learn *not* to do again?** Will you remember this next time the situation arises?
- **What did the setback teach you about yourself?** What strengths did it bring out in you? What weaknesses did it alert you to?
- **What did the setback teach you about other people?** What did you learn about specific people, and what did you learn about people in general?

Why *collecting*, as well as reflecting? Memories are short. If we don't capture useful thoughts and experiences, they tend to fade away in the mists of time. It is worth spending even just a few minutes on the act of *writing down* your answers to questions along the lines of the list given above. The act of putting your thoughts into words helps you reflect a lot more deeply. Your words can then stay as a permanent reminder of your thoughts about what you learned from each setback.

▶ Next, the skills

Your final year is your last chance before graduating to add new skills to your repertoire, before taking your skills (as well as your qualifications) onto the road towards your next job. Whether you're heading for research, or for employment, or don't yet know which, there are many useful skills you can hone and polish during your final year. Many of these can be addressed in tandem with your main agendas of getting your degree successfully and making yourself marketable. Skills which potential employers (and potential research supervisors) admire and want in you include the following:

- **Written communication skills.** Not just in formal essays, reports, dissertations and so on, but in everyday formats such as letter writing, memo writing and email communication.
- **Oral communication skills.** Such as giving a presentation, talking people through an exhibit or poster, developing your interview technique, and so on.
- **Listening skills.** You can set out to develop these quite deliberately. Everyone likes a good listener. In small group situations like tutorials, practise your listening skills for at least some of the time. Don't just think of what *you* want to say next, or listen to what the expert (tutor) says, but listen carefully to the questions that other students ask. You'd be amazed how often one student asks a question that someone else has already asked as a result of not having been listening!
- **Learning skills.** Your learning won't stop when you've got your degree and are into your first job thereafter. That is just the start of much more learning. Since you have to learn a lot in your final year in any case, take the opportunity to think about *how* you learn best. Try out different approaches to managing your own learning, and find out what works well for you, and what does not.
- **Time management skills.** You'll need these for the rest of your life, and there's no better time to sharpen them up than when you're hard pressed and busy. Look at ways you can cut down the amount of time you spend on a task without significantly affecting how well you

complete it. Look at ways of getting, and staying, ahead of your *own* targets, and set these ahead of anyone else's expectations of you.

- **Task management skills.** These overlap with time management skills, but are different too. Task management can be about working on several different things at once. It's about keeping several balls in the air at the same time. Your final year is an ideal occasion to develop such skills, as you have indeed several different kinds of agenda to work with concurrently.

- **Self-management skills.** In your first year there may have been quite a lot of spoonfeeding going on. In your final year, your studying and learning will be very much up to you. You're in control now of all the important things, not least getting ready to be employable. Your final year is the time when you've got the most opportunity to develop yourself as an autonomous learner. Develop yourself as a *thinker*. Employers do indeed want people who will do what they're told, when necessary, but they value even more people who can think for themselves as well as follow instructions, and who know *when* to do which!

- **Interpersonal skills.** Employers (and research supervisors) prefer to take on people who can get on with those around them. Use any time you have working in groups with fellow students to take stock of your interpersonal skills. Think about them too in your everyday social life. Try to become better at working with other people. Develop your own leadership skills in any opportunities you have to do so. Also develop your corresponding 'followership' skills at times when other people are leading. Good followers are much in demand!

- **People management skills.** These are closely related to the interpersonal skills mentioned above, but with a difference: influencing the ways that other people behave. You will already have developed such skills in your relationships with fellow students and tutors, but you may not have been consciously thinking about how what *you* think, say and do influences how others think and react.

What evidence can I build to illustrate my skills?

However sensible it is to use your final year to develop yourself, it's not much good if *you* are the only person who knows what you've developed. For each of the skills you target, identify how you would justify to someone else that you have developed them. Get used to explaining your achievements to other people. This is good practice for convincing employers or others that you're not a solitary, studious individual, but an outgoing, studious individual. Think of gathering your evidence as adding 'frills' to your skills, to make them more visible and attractive.

There are various channels which you can use to assemble your evidence of your skills. These include:

- building a collection of evidence of your work, both at university and outside academia, to show your potential to prospective employers;
- collecting examples of people's opinions (good ones, of course) of your work, such as feedback from tutors on the evidence that you're most proud of;
- getting yourself sufficiently well known (for the best reasons) to people whom you may approach to speak (or write) on your behalf (your referees);
- practising so that you can give a convincing account of yourself when talking to potential employers or research supervisors, whether in formal interviews or in informal chats;
- making sure that your CV creates a good impression of you as a skilled individual, and not just as a well-qualified one;
- not getting so caught up in your studies (or your job hunting) that you lose track of just who you really are, and all the things you've got going for you.

It's all too easy to think about the things you haven't yet done, and become blinded to the strengths that you can display. Keep reminding yourself of the positive sides of your work, and your skills, and your personality. If your strengths are close to the surface of your mind, you'll display them well.

We'll return in more detail to the evidence you can collect, and how to collect it systematically and strategically, later in this chapter. But first, let's look in detail at just one area of skills – that connected with computers, word processing, electronic communication and the Internet.

▶ Become a globalized learner

What is a 'globalized learner'? This term is indeed something quite new. Even when some of your present lecturers were students, no one thought of the extent to which computers and electronic communication could revolutionize life. You *need* to be computer literate nowadays to survive. A university is no longer a relatively self-contained universe. Staff and students no longer keep up with what's going on around the world solely by travelling to conferences (though this is still a highly useful and enjoyable part of professional life for most lecturers). You can find out a great deal about the state of the art in your subject areas just by sitting at a computer linked to the Internet or World Wide Web. You can tune in to up-to-the-minute information about research developments in just about every discipline, from all over the world. You can download information, print it out, store it, write all over it, or you can store information on your own computer or disks, and work with it, reshape it, edit it, and so on.

You may already be highly computer literate. Many students gain great skills with computers simply through playing with them, and enjoying computer games, then perhaps composing or adapting some of these, and so on. Most students are highly 'mouse-trained'! Many students have already gained considerable competence at finding their way round the Internet before they even come to university. You're likely to have further developed such skills during your time at university so far. You may well have been required to conduct Internet searches, and find out which search engines are fastest for finding web sites relevant to your discipline areas. You may well also have been asked to review the *quality* of information on web sites, and to think about the validity and reliability of such information, and to compare this to that of published information in respected journals in the field.

You'll know that it can take a year or two to get a new research development into print in a good journal, but it takes only minutes to put it up on the Web. You'll also know that much of the material on the Web is un-refereed, and perhaps quite invalid, but that among all the dross are diamonds: new ideas that people have generously put up for anyone to see, rather than holding them back for a major publication. Of course, it's not always sheer generosity that motivates such actions; getting an idea on the Internet can be a way of putting a time mark on the date of making the discovery, which can establish who was first to do so.

Being skilled at using computers is quite central to many disciplines. If you're into computer-aided design, for example, you'll need to have mastered complex software packages to turn your ideas into designs. In many mathematical subject areas (for example in disciplines such as science and engineering), you may need to use computers to do complex calculations, modelling, and simulations which simply could not be done in a reasonable timescale by any other means. You may be using computers to help you to analyse, interpret and present practical data and measurements.

You may also be using electronic communication to keep in contact with members of your own class, and with tutors, and with friends elsewhere. You may be submitting some coursework assignments to your tutors electronically, and receiving feedback from them in the same way.

It's worth becoming a globalized learner, not just for its own sake, but also because employers want to recruit such people. They want their organizations to be up to date. Research supervisors want students who are able to keep an electronic eye on what's going on elsewhere, and can communicate new findings quickly when appropriate.

There are, however, dangers. For example, if you've got Internet access on your own machine, it's tempting to spend far too long surfing the net.

(It's not so easy to get carried away if you are on a general access machine in a computer laboratory, learning resources centre or library, as sooner or later the pressure of other people wanting access to the machine will stop you.) There's nothing at all wrong with surfing. It's a really good way to find out all sorts of things you wouldn't have found out about by any other means. But this is your final year. Your time is at a premium. You just cannot afford to spend large amounts of time on things which don't contribute towards your objectives for this one-off situation. The problem takes forms such as:

- It's tempting to start surfing as a work avoidance strategy, when you're doing something particularly hard, or boring!
- Once you start surfing, it's hard to stop and get back to real work.
- Time flies when you're enjoying yourself, and you may well have no idea how long you've spent drifting around the Internet.

There are, as always, sensible tactics which can add up to a strategy for making good use of computers and electronic communication. Take your pick from the following ideas. Work out which (if any) of them are particularly relevant to you:

- Use the Internet as 'reward time'. Earn each spell of playing with the Internet by doing a solid, important study-related task *first*, or a useful job-hunting-related one.
- Plan your use of the Internet, at least sometimes! In other words, go into the Internet with a definite purpose. Decide what you're wanting to find out, and use the technology to narrow down your search until you've found exactly what you're looking for.
- Make a learning log now and then when you use the Internet. I don't mean write down everything you did, and everything you found! Just spend a couple of minutes thinking back to what worked well, what was useful, what led nowhere, and so on, and finding out that little bit more about the relationship between you and the electronic world out there.
- Write shorter emails. If you're using email a lot to communicate with students, tutors, friends, whoever, it's best to keep communications short and relevant. If you're writing shorter emails, you'll be spending less time on them. Besides, people are far more likely to *read* short emails than long ones!

But what if I'm starting from scratch?

If you happen not to be one of those students who has already got into email, word processing or using the Internet, much of what I said above could seem like a foreign language. I've therefore added some 'getting started' tips below. If you're already into computers and electronic communication, skip these – or better, scan them just in case there's the occasional point you hadn't found out for yourself.

Getting started with word processing

It's useful to develop word-processing skills. Even if you've not done this before your final year, it's not too late to start, especially if you've got access to your own computer (and even better, a printer as well). Working with word processors can almost be relaxing, compared to learning things for your final exams. The process of writing a final-year research report or dissertation can usefully be coupled with learning or improving your word processing. The ability to do your own word processing can mean you don't have to find (and pay!) someone else to produce your CV for you, and could allow you to produce your own thesis if you go in for a higher degree. I've included some straightforward suggestions below, adapted from those I wrote with Steve McDowell in *500 Computing Tips for Trainers* (McDowell and Race 1999). These tips assume that you've already got a basic understanding of word processing, and that your software includes the most common refinements present in modern packages. All of these suggestions are designed to save you time in the long run. None takes long to experiment with.

- **Explore the different options you have for selecting text.** The mouse (or trackpad) is very useful for selecting text – for example to move, copy or delete it. Other techniques, such as double-clicking, clicking in margins and dragging are very useful and less well-known. They can make selecting and modifying text much faster. Load a document, save it as something else (so that you don't lose the original), and play with the various options until you find out which you prefer, and trust yourself to use them all.
- **Find out for yourself how text can be deleted accidentally.** A common problem that beginners have is that they select some text and then type something. The selected text is then replaced by what they have typed. This can be useful when it's exactly what you *intend* to do, but beginners often have trouble with work 'disappearing' because of this. Delete some text this way deliberately, then use the 'undo' command to recover it.
- **Have a look at the non-printing characters in a document.** Most word processors allow you to show characters such as spaces and carriage returns that aren't printed and don't normally show on the screen. Making these visible can help you to understand why the computer is behaving the way that it is.

- **Practise rearranging a document.** It is very easy to select text and change a document's font or size, its alignment or its colour. This makes it easy to produce a range of styles. Try altering fonts, and see which look best for the sort of document you're likely to produce most often. For assessed coursework, make sure you use fonts that are easy to read! Try altering margins by changing the page setup. Experiment with single spacing between lines, double spacing and 1.5-line spacing. The latter is often easiest to read for essays or reports. Double spacing may be asked for by lecturers, however, to leave them more room to write comments on your work. If they have asked for double spacing, they really mean it!

- **Develop familiarity with cut, copy and paste.** By selecting text and then cutting it, copying it or pasting it into another place, documents can be modified easily. These techniques are also useful for entering text repeatedly. It is often possible to use keyboard commands for these functions and this can be faster than using the mouse to access menus.

- **Become expert at the use of headers and footers.** These add information automatically to all the pages in a document. The information can include page numbers and the date as well as any text of your choice. Don't, however, go overboard. Too much in running headers or footers tends to detract from your main text on a page.

- **Use numbering and bulleting to help to clarify some documents.** It is easy to add numbers or bullets to lists. Paragraphs can even be numbered or bulleted automatically as you type them. Select a list of separate points, and explore the bulleting and numbering options in your word-processing package. Use the 'undo' and 'redo' commands to help you observe exactly what happens each time you make a change.

- **When you want to indent text, use the 'tab' key, or alter the page setup using the 'ruler' at the top of your screen.** Most fonts used on word processors are proportional. This means that if spaces are used to indent text, correct alignment may be impossible. Even if indenting looks correct on the screen, it may print out incorrectly. Practise indenting selected paragraphs in a document.

- **Find out how to use borders around paragraphs.** Borders are very good for separating sections of text, or for emphasizing key information (for example, the principal conclusions in a report). Find out how to put lines around selected text, how the lines can be modified in thickness or colour, and how they can be turned on and off.

- **Explore for yourself the benefits and dangers of spell and grammar checkers.** Spell checkers are very useful for finding errors, but they have major limitations. They only check words that are in their dictionary: they can't check for missing or wrong words. They can't distinguish between common errors where the wrong word is used, such as 'their' or 'there', 'principal' or 'principle', 'its' and 'it's'. Grammar checkers can help with finding errors but they can also lead to a very restricted style of writing. No one I know uses an electronic grammar checker! Human beings are still much better at giving you feedback about your grammar.

- **Get some safe practice at global editing.** For example, take a floppy disk with a word-processed document file on it, and save the file as something else straightaway, so the original one is safe. With your 'something else' file, global edit selected words, or punctuation markings, such as 'was' to 'is', 'were' to 'are', 'double quotes' to 'single quotes' and so on. Also play with aspects of the document layout, for example by changing all multiple spaces to single spaces between words and sentences. It can also be very useful to change each 'manual line break' to a space – for example when inserting some scanned-in text into an existing document. Once more, explore how the 'undo' command can rescue you when you've done some global editing you don't want!

- **Find out how to make good use of the 'find . . . replace' command.** This can be useful when you remember making a mistake, but have forgotten where it was in the document. It is also useful to dump something unusual (xxx, &&, ppp, and so on) at points in a long document that you may want to return to quickly, and just use the 'find' command to return immediately to such points. It is best that such anomalous oddities are such that they would be picked up by the spell checker facility later, if you happen to forget about them! Don't enter them into your 'custom dictionary' or you won't be able to find them again!

- **Use 'autocorrect' to enter repeated terms quickly.** Autocorrect is designed to correct frequent typing errors (such as 'teh' instead of 'the'). You can enter your own corrections and autocorrect can also be used to enter long words quickly. As an example, imagine that you are typing the word 'substantiate' frequently in a document. If you tell autocorrect to replace 's' with substantiate, every time you type 's' the full word will appear. Remember that, in this example, it is 'space-s-space' that is being replaced by 'substantiate'. You wouldn't want to replace all the occurrences of the letter 's' in your document! You can even do autocorrection for complete phrases, such as 'ict' becoming 'information and communication technologies'. It is important, of course, to make sure that you don't end up with a nonsense phrase creeping into ordinary language. The 'undo' facility can be used to undo single instances of an autocorrect modification – for example, if you *really* want say 'ict'.

- **Don't worry about all the unnecessary complications.** For example, most word-processing packages can perform 'mail merge' operations, suitable for adding name and address details to letters to a list of different people. You are unlikely to need this facility, so don't bother to learn about it – you don't have the time!

Getting into email

Email is the simplest form of communicating by computer. Electronic communication is addictive! For most people who have already climbed the learning curve of finding out how to use email, the apprehension they may have experienced on their first encounter has faded into insignificance. The Internet lets users anywhere in the world exchange messages. Once you are connected to the Internet, sending email is cheaper than sending a letter or making a telephone call and is much quicker. Using email can be a useful distraction and provide a welcome break between serious study tasks during your final year. You may already be skilled at email – if not, the following suggestions may help you to get started.

- **Remind yourself that you're extremely unlikely to break the computer!** While learning how to use email, the only thing you are likely to risk is losing some of the work you have done with the machine, and even this risk is quite small, with 'undo' commands in most computer software.
- **You don't have to send an email message until you're completely happy with it.** This allows you to edit and polish your writing. If you were to attempt this much editing on a handwritten message, it would either look very messy, or have to be written out several times before the same amount of adjustments had been achieved.
- **Regard email as environment-friendly.** The saving of paper can be significant. If the computing facilities are already available, it can be argued that using email incurs negligible costs.
- **Use email to keep in touch with some of your friends elsewhere.** This becomes a good reason for logging on in the first place, and may get you to the library, or to your own machine, and increase the possibility of you doing some useful work while you're there.
- **Find out what email facilities your university has available.** It may be possible for you to use these facilities, saving you the effort of organizing your own. If you're lucky enough to have your own computer linked to a service provider, you can use email both in college and at home, and send messages and files between the two addresses.
- **Take care to let people know if your email address changes.** If you move from one service provider to another, for example, or if your institution changes its address details, your email address will change. It is worth emailing everyone in your address book with details of any forthcoming change, and then emailing them from your new address again as soon as the change is implemented.
- **Ask other people if they have email and what their addresses are.** Most email software includes an electronic address book. You can enter email addresses into it when you are told them. When you want to

send an email message you can just select who you want to send it to and the computer will fill the address in for you.

- **Collect your email frequently and reply quickly.** If you don't collect your email frequently and respond promptly you will lose out on the benefits of fast communication and other people will be less inclined to send you email in future.
- **Make most messages really brief and to the point.** Few people take much notice of long email messages. If a message is longer than one screen, most readers either dump it or file it. Make good use of the medium, and aim to send several short messages rather than try to cram lots of points into a single missive.
- **Take particular care with your email message titles.** It can take ages to search for a particular email if it is not clear what each message is about. The computer software can sort messages by date, and by sender, but it is more time consuming to use it to track down topics. Two or three well-chosen keywords make the most useful titles.
- **Send more detailed messages as attached files.** If you want to send more detailed communications, you can produce them in another, more flexible computer package. If you save the file you produce, you can then send it with a short email message explaining what you are sending.
- **Make use of mailing lists to send copies to more than one recipient at the same time.** Most email software makes it very simple to send extra copies of a message to other people. It is also often possible to create lists, or groups, of people and to send messages to all the members of a group at the same time. These groups can also be saved for future mailings.
- **Don't place too much trust on email.** Messages and files sometimes don't get through, and you don't always find out that this has happened. You only *know* that a message has reached its intended recipient when you receive a reply. Some students have emailed assignments to tutors who haven't received them, and have ended up missing assessment deadlines as a result – not the sort of thing you want to happen in your final year. With anything important, start your email along the lines of 'please confirm straightaway that this has reached you'.

Getting started with the Internet

The Internet is the electronic highway to the largest collection of information and data ever constructed by the human species. There is information available via the World Wide Web on every imaginable subject. Playing with the Internet is easy, but *learning* from it is not always straightforward. The following suggestions may help you to not only enjoy playing with the Internet, but also to develop your techniques so that you learn effectively from it too.

- **Choose your times carefully.** If you intend to retrieve information from the Internet during the day, choose a time when the system is not too congested. When the system is busy, it becomes very slow and communications can even break down. If possible, use the Internet when the USA is asleep (in the mornings for UK users).
- **Use 'local' sources when possible.** A number of organizations have sites in different parts of the world. If you can find one in the same country (or even continent) that you are working from, communications can be faster at busy times.
- **Use a good search engine to help you find information.** There are quite a few search engines available on the Internet. Choose one that performs quickly and produces a good range of results. Once again, some search engines have sites in different parts of the world, so using a 'local' one may be faster.
- **Learn to use the advanced facilities of a search engine to refine searches.** Simple searches on almost any single word produce too many matches to be useful. Search engines usually allow you to carry out more refined searches in order to home in more accurately on the information you are looking for. Many of these engines include tutorials that will help you to use them effectively.
- **Be cautious about the quality of the information available on the Internet.** It is very cheap and easy to set up pages, particularly on the World Wide Web. As a result, the quality of the information is very variable. Before using it, check out the reliability of the source of the information. The information could have been put there by students as a prank, by a fundamentalist group or by a company for sales purposes. Ideally, you should only use information that provides some means (such as references) of verifying it.
- **Acknowledge your sources of information.** If you use information from an Internet source in your coursework, for example, you should give the address of the page where it was found. This enables the source to be verified and prevents you from being accused of plagiarism.
- **Don't forget where you've been.** Depending on your software, you will be able to add 'bookmarks' or 'favourites' which will mark the pages that are most important to you. You can only do this, however, when working on your own machine, as if you're using a networked public-access terminal, everyone else's bookmarks will be there too.
- **Strike a sensible balance between playing with the Internet and learning from it.** It is perfectly natural, and healthy, to explore and follow up interesting leads, even when they take you far away from the purpose of your searches. However, it is useful to develop your skills to ration the amount of random exploration, and to devote 'spurts' of conscious activity to following through the specific purposes of searches.

How can I emerge as a highly-skilled, highly-trained individual – and with a degree?

Let's get back now to the central issue of balancing your act during your final year. There are indeed all manner of things you need to achieve *besides* getting your degree. Many of these have been mentioned in this chapter already. But you must make sure that you don't get carried away with becoming that highly-skilled, highly-trained individual, and put so much energy and time into it that you end up without the degree. Employers do indeed want competent people, but they will have plenty of *well-qualified*, competent people to choose from. Make sure that you aim for the well-qualified bit too! Never forget that your future salary will depend to some extent on being well-qualified.

Think, just for a moment, of some of the things that may depend on your future salary. They include your future lifestyle, the sort of place you'll live in, the sort of car you'll drive, the sort of leisure activities you'll be able to pursue, the sort of people who will be part of your social life, and so on. But money is far from being everything. More important, the range of jobs that you can choose from depends on having something academic to show for your time at university. Much more important, your job satisfaction depends upon having the freedom and scope to get into something that will really suit you, and that depends upon being well-qualified, as well as being attractive to employers. However well you've honed your skills profile, you need to be sufficiently well-qualified to get onto those job shortlists.

The moral of this is clear enough. Even if you *enjoy* all the steps you'll need to take in your final year to become a well-rounded, skilled individual, attractive to potential employers, and with good career prospects, you're at university to get qualified too. Sometimes, getting your degree will involve harder work than any of the other things we've been exploring in this chapter. You still need to tackle this hard work. You still need to make sure that the hard work you do has good pay-off towards getting your degree.

What else can pave the way to my future, over and above my degree results?

We've looked at some of the things that employers like. I've stressed, now and then, that you need to be systematic and strategic in collecting *evidence* of your well-rounded personality, and of the range of your job-related competences (or indeed, research-related competences). There are three main ways that you can demonstrate to the world that you're a good investment for employers: visible evidence, vocal evidence, and vicarious evidence.

Visible evidence

This can take the form of a portfolio of your achievements. Such a portfolio may be an expanded version of your CV containing artefacts rather than just details. There's no single formula for your portfolio – it's meant to be *about* you, designed *by* you, showing what *you* want to present about yourself. Some of the things that could go into your portfolio include: exhibits of your work, such as drawings, paintings, sculptures, plans, designs, drafts, well-chosen examples of essays, reports, assignments, and so on. It is wise not to put too many examples of the same sort in your portfolio. You want it to reflect the *breadth* and *range* of your skills and competences, not just how many times you've worked on the same sorts of evidence.

Vocal evidence

This is the story you can tell about yourself, your background, your ambitions, your goals and what makes you tick. I've called this 'vocal' evidence because we're thinking this time of what you can tell, rather than what you can show. You may indeed wish to link your vocal evidence to your visible evidence, and practise talking about exhibits from your portfolio. Having a good tale to tell is only half the battle; the other half is becoming skilled and confident at telling it. There are no substitutes for practice and feedback. Tell your tale to yourself in a mirror. Rehearse your tale silently to yourself during time that could otherwise be wasted – on journeys, in boring parts of lectures, while waiting in queues and so on. Rehearse your tale vocally when there are people around who can give you feedback on the impression you make. Make good use of fellow students for this, and play your part and give them feedback on their accounts of themselves.

Vicarious evidence

This is what other people think about you. It can include testimonies from people who know (and like) selected parts of your work, and indeed the whole person that is *you*. Some evidence of this sort will be needed in formal contexts such as references for job applications, but it is still worth building your collection of further evidence from other people. Your file of other people's commentaries on you can include letters of thanks, expressions of appreciation and indeed anything that proves that significant others value you, your work and your skills. This evidence may well form part of the visible evidence in your portfolio, but needs to be seen as separate from what *you* say about yourself.

Other sources of evidence of your skills

Much of the evidence which you need to build up and polish during your final year will be closely connected with your course. This is the time to draw together as many strands as you can. You will probably have at least one of the following to capitalize upon:

- one or more work placements which you may have done at some time in your course;
- part-time or full-time jobs which you may have held down during vacations or alongside your studies;
- voluntary work which you may have done;
- activities outside the academic world of your university, such as in clubs, student union societies, local organizations and so on;
- extra activities inside your academic world, such as being a student representative on a course board or committee;
- special interests or hobbies you have pursued actively alongside your studies or during vacations.

Work placements can be a rich source of additional evidence for you. For a start, there may be documentary evidence that you were a successful member of a team or organization for a significant period of time. This could illustrate your interpersonal skills, and show future employers that you can get on with people. Not least, the evidence could show that you proved able to turn up regularly and on time for work, and that you did a good job when you got there. Workplace supervisors and others who may have known that side of you may be able and willing to be referees for job applications you make during your final year. They may even be able to suggest employment opportunities that might interest you. A significant number of students return, after getting their degrees, to an organization where they did a work placement.

Similar considerations apply to part-time or full-time jobs of any kind that you've held during your earlier time at university or in vacations. All sorts of secondary evidence about your character and abilities can arise from such jobs. For example, if you have been in charge of money, or resources, or other people's work, it says a lot about you being trustworthy, responsible and employable. Skills that you learned for these jobs may be transferable to future full-time employment situations.

If you spent some of your time (and perhaps still manage to do so) on voluntary work of some kind, you have immediate evidence that you can put other people's needs first. You may have some documentary evidence of having helped people successfully – letters of appreciation and so on. If your voluntary work involved disabled or disadvantaged people, you will necessarily have developed skills and attitudes which are likely to reflect a caring human being – someone who is also going to be an employee who brings credit to a firm or organization.

Involvement in student societies and clubs is also a source of useful evidence. For example, if you acted as secretary it shows that you were trusted to work with words, write minutes, prepare agendas, contribute to meetings, and so on. All of these skills may be required, and desired, by future employers. If you were elected to the chair of a society, it shows that other people believed in your ability to act as a leader and to manage other people in the context of meetings. If you've been treasurer to any organization it shows that you were trusted with other people's money, and that you were believed to be sufficiently responsible to keep track of it and oversee its expenditure.

You may have spent some time abroad, either on study-related or hobby-related activities. This is evidence of further key skills development – organizing your own life, perhaps learning another language, fitting in with another culture and so on.

Your own hobbies and leisure interests can tell a positive story to employers. The simple fact of being *really* interested in something shows you're not just someone who drifts round and does nothing. It is normal to include at least some detail of hobbies and leisure interests on CVs. At most job interviews, someone will ask you to say a little more about some of these. When you reply to such questions, your enthusiasm can come across vividly, and your confidence while answering such questions will be high – you're likely to know far more about this subject than anyone else present at your interview. The impressions of enthusiasm and confidence are likely to be retained by your interviewers, and may well influence their selection decision positively.

▶ What about the thrills?

In this chapter we've been looking at:

- spills (setbacks, problems, pressures);
- skills (not just academic ones, but life skills and work skills);
- frills (visible evidence of the well-developed human being you are).

There are plenty of thrills too! Some of these are obvious: doing really well in an important exam, giving a good interview and being offered a job, and so on. Some of the spills are thrills too, if you look at them in a constructive, reflective way. It's even a thrill, in its own way, simply to *be* in your final year. Not everyone gets that far. Not everyone steps back from it, as you are doing, and puts it into perspective. Not everyone develops a collection of tactics to build into a strategy for tackling it. Not everyone reminds themselves (as I trust you did in the 'diamond-9' exercise near the beginning of this book) of the rationale underpinning their final year. Aren't you just a little bit thrilled that you're already tackling your final year that bit more systematically?

Personal action plan

Summarize your thoughts, and action points, from this chapter by jotting down your own responses to the questions below.

Was your worst nightmare about your final year real or imaginary?

What do you now think is the most important 'spill' that you need to plan to avoid?

What's your intention, now, regarding making setbacks (when they happen) useful?

How do you rate yourself at this point on the various skills discussed in this chapter?

Type of skill	I'm fine at these	I'm adequate at these	I'm going to work on these	I don't need these at this time
Written communication skills, *other* than essay writing, etc.				
Oral communication skills.				
Listening skills.				
Learning skills.				
Time management skills.				
Task management skills.				
Self management skills.				
Interpersonal skills.				
People management skills.				

How are you doing at being a globalized learner? Record your present self-assessment here.

Attribute	This is me!	This is sometimes me	I'm working towards this	I'm not going to do this
I use computers as my main work-avoidance strategy!				
I use computers as a welcome break from work.				
I'm well-practised with word processing.				
I'm quick at typing.				
I have good document layout skills.				
I'm proficient with email.				
I'm an able surfer of the Internet.				
I'm good at being systematic at information retrieval from the Internet.				
I'm good at downloading and processing information from the Internet.				

Jot down two of your best pieces of *evidence* to show future employers that you're worth taking on:

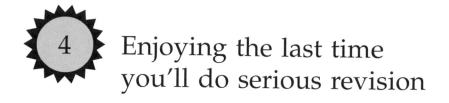

Enjoying the last time you'll do serious revision

▶ A big, important task

As far as your academic success is concerned, revision is the most import-ant study activity you will do in your final year. The quality of your degree will depend on the *quality* of your revision much more than on the *quantity* of your revision. Revision is almost always for one main goal: to get ready for formal assessment of one kind or another. To have reached your final year you're no stranger to revision. Indeed, you may really enjoy doing it, and be very good at organizing it. Alternatively, you may already have quite a negative feeling about revision. You've probably already used things from the study-skills literature, or attended study-skills lectures or workshops. If so, you'll know that the advice and tactics all seem very sensible at the time, but all too easily get forgotten when the pressure is on. In this chapter I'm not going to repeat all the advice you've heard before, but merely summarize the ideas that I think will be most useful for you to use during this, your last spell of revision.

◉ Task: mixed feelings about revision: which do you share?

Some of the feelings about revision that are common among final-year students are listed below. Let's start this chapter by getting your feelings out into the open. Tick those that apply to you, put two ticks against those that dominate your feelings about revision, and add any particular feelings of your own at the end of the list.

I just love doing revision!	
I dread starting revision, and put off the evil moment as long as I possibly can!	

I feel I'm good at revision, and organize it well.	
Revision is not normal life; I have to shut myself away from my friends, my interests, everything!	
I get into a rut while revising: turning the pages for hours, with nothing really going in.	
I base my revision on practising answering questions for my exams.	
I revise best with fellow students: we quiz each other, and learn a lot from each other.	
I get really worried about how much studying other students may be doing.	
I balance revision with other things, so it doesn't take over my life.	
I start revising really early, so I don't have to do an intense final slog at it.	
I never seem to have enough time left to do all that I would like to do when revising.	
I revise for short spells at a time, and take frequent breaks.	
I can keep my head down, and maintain my concentration, for hours at a time.	
I don't revise on the last night before an exam, saving my energy for the exam itself.	
I stay up into the early hours just before an exam, and remember a lot that way.	

You don't need me to tell you which are the best options to have selected. The main thing is to get plenty of learning pay-off from your revision activities, and not sit there for hours turning pages without anything much happening. For most people, concentration spans are limited, especially when doing something as hard as real learning. This means that it's usually better to work in short spells, with breaks in between. The breaks are most beneficial when they involve a real change – a walk outside, a chat with friends, a catnap – anything to give your brain a rest. Actually, it's not really a rest altogether, as your brain will continue, during these breaks, to make sense of the things you've been learning.

▶ How does the final-year exam system work?

There won't be any real surprises in your final exam *processes*, and there shouldn't be any surprises in the *questions* if you've revised well. To have got this far, you've done countless exams. Your final exams may well count for somewhat more than any you've done so far, but the *processes* are not new. However, your final exams are a one-off chance to get a good degree classification, so there is indeed the chance that you'll feel under a little more pressure than before.

A positive way to look at it is that since final exams are 'more serious', they're usually designed more carefully. Questions on your final exam papers will have to have survived scrutiny by several people, and won't just be the undiluted whims of particular lecturers. The standard of the exams will have been judged to be correct. The marking will be moderated more keenly. Your work could well be double marked. There is every possibility that external examiners may also make judgements about your answers. The increased role of external examiners is perhaps the only real difference between your forthcoming final exams and most of those you've already had.

What may external examiners do?

'External examiners' sound somewhat scary! In fact, they're usually on your side – I'm one, and I am! Their work is to make sure that your assessors are being fair and reasonable. They often look very carefully at borderline cases, and are particularly on the lookout for any candidates who could be moved up over a borderline, rather than trying to move candidates down. They are usually lecturers from other universities, well experienced in the subjects you're taking, and also well practised in making sure that assessment is fair. They also check out the overall standards of courses, comparing those at your university with those elsewhere.

You may meet an external examiner or two yourself. They often take part in viva exams, where they talk to a range of candidates. Sometimes their role is to check out that matter of borderlines, and having a viva can sometimes take you up and over a borderline. It is rare for a viva to take you downwards. External examiners are usually testing the course, rather than testing you. At a viva, they are likely to be looking for how well the subject has been taught, and how fairly it has been assessed, more than how well you as an individual have learned from it.

▶ Working out what not to do this time!

In the task earlier in this chapter, you may already have reminded your-self of some of the good (and bad) habits upon which the quality of your revision can depend. This year is probably the last time you'll have revision, on this scale, to tackle. Even if you subsequently study for higher degrees or professional qualifications, and prepare for yet more exams, it will never feel quite the same as it does now. Then, you're much more likely to be revising a narrower field very deeply. Now, you're tackling a range of subjects and topics, and needing to balance your time and energy sensibly between them. Now, you need to be kind to yourself, but at the same time make sure that in this important revision scenario you give it your best shot.

It's worth remembering that even though final exams are important, you need to be fit and well (and not tired and exhausted) to do yourself justice in them. Revision is important, but not as important as saving enough energy to tackle your exam questions well. You're directly meas-ured on how well you answer your exam questions; no one can directly measure how well you've revised.

Work out your revision strategy now. A sensible revision strategy is not just a collection of good intentions, it's a combination of tactics – practical, achievable steps building into a coherent whole strategy. The following suggestions are to remind you of the revision tactics that have proved, for most students, to be the safest and most productive. Choose which of these suggestions you will include as tactics in your strategy. Congratulate yourself on those you're already including.

Tactical tips for revision: processes and planning

- **Start early.** Start today if you've not already done so – you're bound to have something that you can revise. Don't put off starting. It doesn't feel good to put it off! You may as well break the ice and make that first move. Even just half an hour is the difference between having started and not yet having started.
- **Look carefully at the learning pay-off of each approach you use.** How much are you really learning? Just reading your notes, textbooks and papers is not much use. This has low learning pay-off. It's better to turn your materials into questions that you can use to test yourself. At

the end of the day, you'll be measured on your ability (and speed) at answering questions. Practising answering questions has high learning pay-off, and is a directly relevant revision tactic.

- **Spend at least some of your revision time working with fellow students.** You can learn a lot from them (and they from you). You deepen your own understanding of things each time you explain them to someone else. Working with other students also helps you to keep an eye on how your learning is going compared to theirs. If you find yourself well ahead, this improves your own confidence. If you find yourself lagging behind in some topics, it at least lets you know where you need to direct some more time and energy. In any case, it's more sociable to work with other students than to spend all of your revision time in solitary confinement. It's more like normal life!

- **Work in short spells, not long slogs.** When you're using tactics that involve high learning pay-off, as suggested above, your brain tires quite quickly. Conversely, if you can stick at something for hours, it's unlikely that it is delivering high learning pay-off to you. Don't spend longer than half an hour, or three-quarters at the most, on a single element of revision. Take a break. Do something entirely different. The breaks don't have to be long. Fifteen minutes can be enough. Turn mealtimes into breaks.

- **A change is nearly as good as a rest.** Don't stick too long at revising the same topic. Switch to something entirely different for a while, then come back to the first topic. In the time in between, your brain will still have been processing what you learned about the first topic, and it often seems easier when you return to it than it was when you left it.

- **Map out your revision time.** Don't spend *hours* doing this – that would be a revision-avoidance strategy! However, it is worth spending a little time making sure that you are splitting up your available time in such a way that all the topics you need to study are included in sensible proportions.

- **Budget your time according to your need.** Allow more time for the topics that you're not too hot on, and less time for things you already know well. In your final exams, you should aim to have as much choice as possible, so it's worth polishing up those areas that you're weaker at, as well as keeping your best topics up to scratch.

- **Make your revision timetable really flexible.** Include planned time off. You can't revise all the time, so you shouldn't try to. When you're taking a *planned* afternoon off, or even a planned weekend off, you can enjoy it far more, because it's part of your strategy rather than an escape from revision.

- **Plan in some 'any other business' time.** This is time where you've planned to do some revision, but you haven't planned in advance exactly what. This time can be really valuable for catching up on those topics that are taking longer to get to grips with than you'd anticipated. Alternatively, you can use it sometimes to give an extra polish to some things you already know well.

- **Keep track of what works well for you.** Use your revision as a mini research project about how *you* learn best, and indeed how you learn badly! Find out as much as you can about the processes which are best for you, and increase your use of these tactics. It's worth spending around five minutes a day just thinking about which revision processes worked best that day, and why. These five minutes can save you an hour or two the next day.

▶ What about the rest of your life?

One answer is that you've got the rest of your life for the rest of your life. That's probably not the answer that you're hoping for, however. In fact, the more you can make your final revision weeks and months 'relatively normal', the better your chances of sticking to a sensible strategy, using productive tactics. There may be some things that you need to spend less time on, and some that you can safely put on hold during this important stage of your life. The time when you're doing your final revision is not the best time to completely change your lifestyle in any way. It's *not*, for example, the best time to:

- give up smoking;
- give up drinking entirely;
- abandon entirely your favourite sport;
- become a hermit;
- start a really important new relationship;
- move home;
- become vegetarian;
- change religion;
- lose two stones on a diet;
- decide to run marathons for the first time.

In short, the best thing you can do about the rest of your life, while revising, is keep it as normal as is reasonably possible. Do most of the normal things, but for less of the total time, so that you can fit in the business of revision, and also leave time for the job-hunting necessities as and when they arise. Doing your revision well is paving the way towards the rest of your life.

When job-hunting activities *need* to be accommodated during your revision time, they too are part of preparing for the rest of your life. As far as is reasonably possible, arrange that job-hunting activities don't interfere with your revision, or indeed your exam period itself. If, however, an opportunity that is really important to you comes up in the middle of your revision, you need to be able to follow it up, otherwise you'll wonder for ever whether it might have been a really good opportunity. That's why it is best to plan your revision flexibly, so that you can interrupt it without any real problem, should the need arise. Other circumstances can interrupt revision too, such as family emergencies, becoming ill yourself, and all the other things that are part of normal life. Keep your options open to deal with urgent events, without throwing your revision completely into chaos.

▶ Being a part-time reviser

If you're a part-time student, you'll already know all about being a part-time reviser. Revision has to be accommodated with one or more regular work schedules, family commitments and any of the other competing factors in the life of any part-time student. Even if you're a full-time student, you may well have a part-time job too – or even a full-time one. It could be worth thinking of jacking in your job during the time you'll need for serious revision, but life's not always that simple. You may have your lifestyle to support. You may have other people depending upon you bringing in some earnings while you study. You may have to accept that you're a part-time reviser after all. That's not bad news however; thousands of part-time revisers revise effectively, efficiently and successfully. You can too. In fact, having 24 hours a day for revision isn't ideal for anyone. Only so much real revision can be done in any one day. Boredom sets in if there's too much time, and nothing other than an unending pile of studying to do in it. The other parts of your life can actually help your revision to be more efficient and focused, but *you* need to do your part too.

   If you're a part-time reviser, you need to be doubly sure that the time you spend revising is really productive. You've not got room for poor tactics in your strategy. Go for the tactics that have the highest learning pay-off. In particular, spend some of each day on that vital activity: practising answering questions. You don't have to write all of your answers down; some of them can be *thought* through rather than spelled out. Also spend some of each day researching the questions that you're aiming to become able to answer. If you know all the possible questions, you're in a position to prepare yourself to answer most of them.

▶ Working with a mate

What if you're not living on your own during your final year? Most students aren't. You may be living with a partner, or one or more friends.

Even if you're not living with someone, there are likely to be one or more people you see a lot of, including during the time you spend on vital final revision. Your mate, or flatmates, or housemates, may or may not be fellow students. They may or may not be final-year students themselves. He, she or they may never have been students at all. Or they could be just like you – on the same course, preparing for the same exams and hunting for the same jobs. I've already pointed towards the benefits of doing at least some of your revision with other people. Working with a mate has many potential benefits, but also some significant pitfalls. The following suggestions may help you to maximize the advantages and avoid some of the dangers.

Do:

- **Let your mate right into your life.** For example, if you're a final-year student and your mate isn't, don't shut yourself away in your own world of revision. Friends who are ignored or put aside can vanish. Having something that is a major part of your life but isn't a part of your mate's, can make him or her feel excluded and even unvalued.
- **Use each other to keep each other going.** If your mate is also a student, it can help if you both study at the same time, and share the rewards of relaxation at the same time after you both feel you've earned them. If you're the only one in your final year, you can ask your mate (or friends) to help you out by making it easier for you to get on undistracted, and by giving up some of their time and energy directly to help you revise.
- **Get your mate to quiz you on what you know.** Even someone studying a completely different subject can fire questions at you, if you provide them with the ammunition. Explain to them that it's very good to be put in the position of practising putting across what you already have mastered. It keeps it fresh and topped-up in your brain.
- **Get your mate to quiz you on what you don't yet know.** This is more delicate! If you're asked too much, too often, about what you don't yet know, you can become demoralized. However, a sympathetic mate can keep tabs on the things that you often seem to have problems with, and gently slip questions on these topics in among lots of questions that you have no trouble answering.
- **Reciprocate.** If you're both studying the same discipline, you'll learn just as much by quizzing your mate and judging the answers you're given as from answering questions yourself. Even if you're studying quite different subjects, there are benefits to stepping away from your own revision every now and then. It may seem like the last thing you want to do to spend time asking a mate questions you yourself don't need to know the answers to, but regard it as a mental break from thinking about your own subject.

- **Recruit his or her help directly.** If they care about you, and are not preparing for their own final exams, most friends worth their salt will be only too willing to help. They can look after some of the everyday things such as routine correspondence, paying bills, shopping for food, and so on. They may even be willing to temporarily do more than their share of chores like laundry or housekeeping. The important thing is not to take such help for granted. Be appreciative, and show it.
- **Allow your mate to do really useful things to save you time.** For example, if your mate isn't under pressure, he or she can go to the library for you and locate, borrow and bring back source materials for you. Your mate could hand in that late piece of coursework for you. Your mate could even help you by reading through your dissertation, looking for typographical errors, grammatical slips and checking your referencing for you. This sort of help is best when you have had, or will get, a chance to reciprocate directly.
- **Get your mate to watch out for your stress response levels.** It's so easy to get caught up in the hurly-burly of your final year, and drift further and further away from sensible levels of effort. You can end up not knowing that you are working far too hard to be efficient. Someone else can often tell.

Don't:

- **Lose your mate!** It's dangerously easy to become tetchy, irritable and difficult to live with when you're under a lot of pressure. You may slip towards such behaviour so gradually that you don't notice, but those around you will see it. Listen to anyone who tells you that you're overreacting to minor irritations. Don't snap back, or they'll stop letting you know about this. Many a relationship has broken up during the pressures of final-year revision. But even more final-year students have been *sustained* in this one-off period of time by those closest to them. Remain in the latter category.
- **Make mountains out of molehills.** If you've got a good mate, don't throw all that away if you can't work successfully together at your final-year revision (and perhaps theirs too). If your mate isn't able to be as helpful and supportive as you'd like, keep your patience. If you were to have a major bust-up, it's likely that this in itself would damage your final-year revision far more than just plodding on under less than ideal conditions.
- **End up being blamed for your mate's lack of success.** People who have 'carried someone' through the tough parts of a final year, at cost to themselves, remember this for a long time, and it can permanently damage a friendship or relationship. Similarly, if your mate does a lot to help you in your final-year revision and *you* don't get the result you want or deserve, don't get into a blame culture, don't even *allow* your mate to take any blame.

▶ Core revising and marginal revising

We've looked in some detail at *how* to revise. It is, of course, important to think about *what* to revise. The lecturers who set and mark your exams will each have their own expectations of the nature and amount of back ground reading that they want you to do, and the balance to be struck between this and core subject knowledge and skills.

Whatever you're revising, there will be a range of subject matter of varying importance. The overlapping categories of knowledge and information can be described as follows:

- Core subject knowledge and skills: this will earn you enough credit for a reasonably good degree, but not, on its own, for a distinguished award such as a first-class degree. The core material for your degree will not be vast. It may seem huge, but it's not nearly as big as all the background material which surrounds it. The marks to be gained per hour, studying core material, are reasonably high.
- Background reading: this can make the difference between a reasonable degree and a very good one, but there's an immense amount of background and peripheral material in most subjects. It therefore takes a lot of study hours for every extra mark to be gained.

You'll be encouraged by your tutors to 'read around'. Your revision time is not the best time to follow this advice. If you were going to follow it seriously, you should already have done so by the time you get into final serious revision. Then, you will have distilled much of the background material into concise summaries that lend themselves to being revised. If you're not in this position, now is not the time to wade out into uncharted waters – it will be more valuable to you to concentrate on becoming really expert with the core material. You can then work on scoring some extra marks via your techniques of handling the core material in exams, vivas and so on. Really good written and oral communications skills (not least the ability to read questions really carefully, and focus your answers really clearly) can score just as many marks as could have arisen from a considerable investment of your time and energy in background reading.

▶ Competence and confidence

The more competent you are at showing what you know, the more confident you become about it, the better your morale and the more productive your revision. This is an upward spiral. The reverse is also possible! Let's not talk about being *incompetent* though, that's a very negative word. Let's use the word *uncompetent* meaning 'can't *yet* do' for

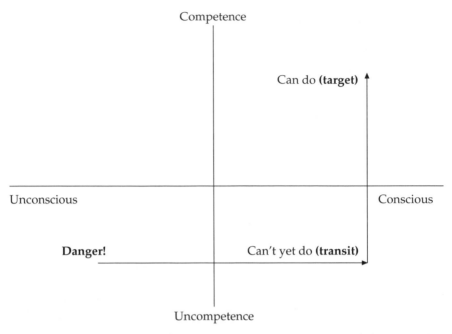

Figure 4.1 Conscious and unconscious competence – and the opposite!

the opposite of competent, meaning 'can do'. Half the battle is *finding out* what you can't yet do. If you know exactly what you can't yet do, you can usually do something about it during your revision.

Let's visualize this. Look at Figure 4.1, and think about the four boxes. 'Conscious competence' is your target. Your revision strategy needs to get all sorts of things into this box.

'Conscious uncompetence' is a very useful step towards conscious competence. When you know exactly what you can't yet do, you're in a strong position to find out how to do it. I've therefore called this the 'transit' box, as most things are easily moved up out of it (except, of course, all of those things which you can't yet do and don't ever *need* to do).

'Unconscious uncompetence' is the danger area. It's the things that you *don't know* that you can't yet do which are the problem. It's not much use just finding out about these when you see the questions on your final exam papers. Effective revision is about digging deep into the 'danger' area. Find out all you can about what you didn't know you couldn't yet do. You can't find this out just by reading about the things you already can do. Your best bet for digging into your 'danger' box is to base most of your revision on *doing* things with your knowledge, and finding out what you can do, and what you didn't know you couldn't do. As soon as you know *what* you can't yet do it becomes a *conscious* uncompetence in your 'transit' box, and is (as before) relatively easy to turn into a conscious competence in your 'target' box.

The top left box in Figure 4.1 is the 'good news' box! Every time you discover something that you can do well, but didn't *know* you could do, it makes you feel even better, and helps with your confidence.

▶ Preparing and practising to show what you know

Your final year culminates in showing what *you* know and can do. Some of this showing is on your own, against the clock, and with an agenda that is unknown to you in advance, for example in formal exams of one kind or another. Showing what you know in your final year can also include your write-up of major pieces of work, such as a project report or a dissertation. In all these cases, as I've said several times in this book, it's what you *show* that earns you credit, not just what you *know*. Indeed, there's a significant danger for final-year students in that they tend to try to build up their knowledge too much, at the expense of their ability to *communicate* that knowledge, in writing and orally.

How best can you improve your technique for showing what you know? As with almost anything else, the key factor is practice. The more you practise writing out answers (however roughly) and speaking out answers (however quickly), the better you can develop your skills to do these things well when it really matters.

Some of your success will depend upon the speed with which you can show what you know. Time-constrained written exams are a case in point. Lots of candidates run out of time during exams, which usually means that they know more than they showed. How can you get up to speed? It's back to practice again. If you've done something ten times you're bound to be faster at it than you were the first time round. If you've written an essay answer to a likely question ten times, you'll write it all the faster if it comes up in the actual exam. But of course it wouldn't be sensible to write the same essay out ten times. It wouldn't be a good use of your time. It would be much better to spend that time planning ten different essays, and stopping with good essay plans, with the order of presentation mapped out. But that would not help with the vital practising of *writing out* an essay. So it could be even better to spend the time writing out two essays, and planning another six.

I've already pressed you to do some of your serious revision with fellow students. Now I'm suggesting that there's some of it you really have to do on your own. You'll do your exams on your own, so the practice that is about showing what you know has to be done on your own for at least some of the time. That's not to say that it isn't useful to do *some* of the practising along with like-minded fellow students, and learn from each other's triumphs and disasters. But at the end of the day you need to feel comfortable delivering your knowledge and skills on your own. The more you've done it, the more comfortable you can expect to feel.

Looking after yourself

Much of this chapter has already been about looking after yourself. Making your revision efficient helps, as this gives you more time to lead a balanced life in between your efforts. Making your revision have high learning pay-off helps, as this gives you a boost to your confidence, and confidence reduces your stress levels more than anything else. Look back to the discussion in Chapter 1 on taking control of your *responses* to stress.

 Personal action plan

Write down three resolutions to yourself that you're going to try to carry out during your final-year revision time:

Are there any things you're determined *not* to do this time?

Jot down your own plans for keeping the rest of your life in order while you're busy with revision:

What are *your* plans to balance out background reading with the more important things you need to get a good grip on?

Try to think of two things that may be lurking in your 'danger' box – things that your conscious mind could have been hiding from you, that *subconsciously* you know you can't yet do!

What are *you* going to do to develop *speed* in showing what you know, in writing, against the clock, in exams?

5 Tackling those final exams

▶ Troubleshooting your exam technique

You've already had enough experience of exams to write one of those books on exam technique. You know the sort of book, all good common sense, but difficult to put into practice. Now's not the time to learn a whole new range of tricks associated with passing exams. Now's the time for doing a bit of systematic reviewing of your technique, and adjusting it where it could make a real difference to your destiny.

 Task: diagnose your exam technique

You might find it useful to diagnose your own position by rating yourself against some or all of the following statements, and then looking back to work out which of these suggest the top three steps on your action plan to improving your technique.

Some elements of a wise approach to doing exams	I'm quite happy with my position on this	It may help a little for me to work on this	It could help a lot for me to work on this
I check the paper really carefully before I start, making sure I know how many questions I've got to answer, how long the exam actually is, whether I've got to attempt a specified number of questions from particular sections, and so on.			

Some elements of a wise approach to doing exams	I'm quite happy with my position on this	It may help a little for me to work on this	It could help a lot for me to work on this
I read the questions really carefully, and slowly, so that I make sensible choices about which questions to tackle, and in which order it will be best for me to tackle them.			
I plan my time logically, so that I have equal time for each question, and some time in hand at the end to read through my entire script, making additions and corrections as I find them.			
While answering each question, I re-read the question every few minutes, to make sure I'm not going off on tangents or drifting away from where most of the marks will be awarded.			
When I'm tackling a question requiring an essay-type answer, I spend a few minutes jotting down a plan for my essay before starting to write it.			
When I'm doing a question I know a lot about, I make sure I don't spend longer on it than I should, so that I leave plenty of time for the other questions.			
I give myself time to *think* rather than spend all of my energy writing down the first thoughts that come into my mind, and I don't let it worry me that other candidates are writing while I'm thinking!			

Some elements of a wise approach to doing exams	I'm quite happy with my position on this	It may help a little for me to work on this	It could help a lot for me to work on this
If I get stuck on any question, for example if there's something I just can't recall, I don't get into a panic, and I move on to another question which I find easier, then return to the original question when the thing I was looking for comes back into my mind in its own time.			
I don't get worried about parts of questions that I can't do, or things I can't remember, and I concentrate on getting all the available marks for the things I *can* do and *can* remember.			
When I'm doing numerical questions, I show enough of my working so that if I make a mistake in a calculation the examiner can see exactly what the mistake was, and give me credit for everything else I did correctly.			
When I've finished the exam, I use all of my remaining time to go back through what I've written, editing and improving my answers as I go.			

Time management and task management against the clock in exam rooms

Most exams are against the clock. The technical term is 'time constrained' exams. Justification for this sort of exam is that real life is often against the clock. You may well think that measuring your performance against the clock is justified *sometimes* but that there's far too much of this sort of measurement in final-year exams. If you think this, I entirely agree with you, but that doesn't help you! What you need to do is to perfect your own technique at being measured against the clock. Let's accept, for the present, that exams measure your time management skills, there and then, in the exam room.

It's not just time management, however, it's task management too. Task management is about focusing really well, in the time available, on the task posed by each and every question. It's about *answering* the question *as set*. It's about scoring as many marks as possible in *each* minute you spend answering each question. It's about avoiding spinning any yarns that aren't going to earn you any marks. It's about *not* spending half an hour on Question 5 only to find then that it would have been much better to have attempted Question 7 instead. Task management also includes balancing the energy you put into creating your answers to the exam questions, and editing and polishing them. Your second thoughts on your answers may be at least as good as your first thoughts. You need physical space in your answers into which to insert your second thoughts, and it is worth leaving such spaces at the end of each answer, and also (unobtrusively) between sections and paragraphs in your answers.

 Task: improving your time management in exams

Explore your own time management approaches to exams. You've had plenty of practice at this to have got as far as your final year, but it's never too late to review your technique, and possibly pick up something which could gain you a better degree. Next you will see two tables – the first relating to a three-hour exam with five questions to answer (for example problems to solve, or short essays, or a mixture of these), and the second relating to three hours with only three questions (essay type) to answer. There are slightly different wrinkles to tackling these exams. Look carefully at the table relating to whichever sort of exam is closest to the ones you're preparing for. As you study the table, congratulate yourself about the things that are already part of your technique – put a tick beside these parts of the table. More importantly, if you notice something that you could usefully *add* to your technique, put a big asterisk beside such points.

Spend time, to save time, at the start of the exam. Spend up to ten minutes, in a three-hour exam, working out your timetable for the exam. Suppose, for the sake of argument, that you've got five questions to tackle in those three hours, and that the exam starts at 0930. Suppose too that there's a free choice – no compulsory questions. Let's also assume that the questions are more or less the same in format. Here is one way that this exam could go:

Time	Activity
09.30–09.40	**Planning your approach.** Reading the whole paper and deciding which questions you'd most like to attempt. Re-reading the questions and working out which your chosen five are going to be. Deciding which of these are *really good* ones for you (where you'll be able to get high marks), which are *quite good* for you (where you'll be able to get at least half the marks), and which you could do if pushed (where you know there are *some* marks you could score). Deciding which questions *not* to think about, or even to re-read (questions on topics you know you're not good at, or haven't revised at all, and so on). Working out which question you're going to answer first, and which one you'll answer second. Mapping out the starting times for your questions (for example, as below). Allow 20 minutes for editing and polishing at the end, then divide the time equally between your five questions. This means three hours, minus 10 minutes (the ones you're spending now), minus the editing and polishing 20 minutes, which comes to two hours 30 minutes. Divide this by five, and you get 30 minutes per question.
09.40–10.10	**Your first question.** Make sure that you don't spend longer than the allotted time on this one. Since it's likely to be a favourite question, the main danger is that it could overrun. You need to remind yourself to watch the clock carefully during your answer. It can be worth being extra concise, especially in descriptive parts of your answer, or in discussion. You'll probably also have time to come back to this question and add some more detail later in the exam.
10.10–10.40	**Your second question.** This one, too, needs clock-watching. You may not have quite so much to say on this question, but you may have to stop and think a little more often, and this takes time.
10.40–11.10	**Your third question.** This is likely to be one where it's easier to stick to your allotted time, as you won't be quite so keen to answer it as the first two.

Time	Activity
11.10–11.40	**Your fourth question.** This one probably won't be quite so easy for you to answer as the ones you've already done. You may have to stop and think even more. You may end up with some time left over, where you've nothing more to add, in which case you can go on to your last question earlier than the time planned.
11.40–12.10	**Your last question.** This is likely to be a question where you're only chasing *some* of the marks – in other words where you're not really expecting to get all of them. It might feel like quite a tough question, but you can be comfortable that your previous four questions should have passed the exam for you already, and anything that you can squeeze out of the present question is a bonus. You may have time left over for this one, after you've done all you can with it, in which case you can move even earlier to the final editing phase below.
12.10–12.30	**Editing and polishing your answers.** Re-read everything, from beginning to end, adding second (often better) thoughts as and when they occur to you. Correct any mistakes you notice. Make sure that what you wrote was exactly what you *meant*, and that your meaning will come across clearly to the examiner. Candidates who do this editing and polishing really well often score *more* (and that means additional) marks in this final stage than they did in any other corresponding amount of time earlier in the exam.

There are many different kinds of time-constrained exam. Next, let's look at the case of three essay-type answers to be written in three hours, again with a choice of topics from the overall paper. With longer answers, it's even more important not to get into the position of finding that you've spent time on a 'wrong' question. More planning is needed, right at the start. The time management for such an exam could look like this:

Time	Activity
09.30–09.50	**Planning your approach.** Reading the whole paper and deciding which questions you'd most like to answer. Deciding which of these are the best ones for you (where you'll be able to get high marks), which could be *quite good*

Time	Activity
	for you (where you'll be able to get at least half the marks), and which you could do if pushed (where you know there are *some* marks you could score).
	Drafting out basic essay plans for the most likely questions. It's useful to do this right at the start of the exam, as this gives you a way of getting ideas that flash through your mind straight into words on paper. This saves you from trying to store them all up in your mind, and makes you feel much more relaxed.
	Working out which question you're going to answer first, and which one you'll answer second.
	Mapping out the starting times for your questions, for example as below. Allow a little longer (25 minutes) for editing and polishing at the end, then divide the time equally between your three questions. This means three hours, minus 20 minutes (the ones you're spending now), minus the editing and polishing 20 minutes, which comes to two hours 20 minutes. Divide this by three, and you get 45 minutes per question.
09.50–10.35	**Your first question.**
	Spend the first five minutes (at least) fleshing out the essay plan that you made at the start of the exam. Brainstorm all of your ideas onto paper, for example in egg-diagram form. In particular, think carefully about which order you're going to tackle the points on your plan – where you'll start, and where you'll finish. If there are nine main points, roughly divide the remaining time so that you've got (say) four minutes per point on average, then try to stick to this as you write paragraphs covering your points.
	Try to leave some space for the editing and polishing you'll do later in the exam. It can be worth leaving a couple of lines between paragraphs. You may not be able to get all your second thoughts into small spaces like this, but at least you'll be able to make clear notes about where in your script you may add extra discussion.
	Make sure that you don't spend longer than the allotted time on this question. Since it's likely to be a favourite question, the main danger is that it could overrun. You'll probably also have time to come back to this question and add some more detail later in the exam.

Time	Activity
10.35–11.20	**Your second question.** As before, spend five to ten minutes fleshing out your essay plan. You'll get more marks for a well-planned, slightly shorter essay than for a poorly-planned, slightly longer one. This one, too, needs clock-watching. You may not have quite so much to say on this question, but you may have to stop and think a little more often, and this takes time.
11.20–12.05	**Your last question.** It's still worth making that essay plan quite carefully before you start. This is likely to be the question where you're only chasing *some* of the marks – in other words where you're not really expecting to get all of them.
12.05–12.30	**Editing and polishing your answers.** Re-read everything, from beginning to end, adding second (often better) thoughts as and when they occur to you. Make sure that what you wrote was exactly what you *meant*, and that your meaning will come across clearly to the examiner.

When you've got an exam where there is a combination of long-answer essay questions, and shorter-answer problem-solving ones, you can easily extend the above ideas for yourself.

▶ Managing your own stress during exams

Some people love exams, and are never happier than when doing them. If you're such a person, you don't need to read this section – except to remind yourself how lucky you are. For most people, exams cause at least some stress. Because you're in your *final* exams, it seems more important. Some people who've never suffered from exam stress before are surprised at how it can creep up on them in their final exams. Let's look at what you can do, there and then in an exam, to take charge of your own stress levels – and to reduce them as and when you may need to.

As discussed earlier in this book (see Chapter 1) stress is about being under pressure, and the feeling of having more to cope with than you've got time or energy to handle. This is, to some extent, exactly the case for most people in most exams. The physical symptoms of this sort of stress are quite common and normal, and can include:

- higher than normal pulse rate;
- faster than normal breathing;
- sweating;
- anxiety;
- upset stomach;
- (add your own particular symptoms here, to remind you of what you need to confront).

Such symptoms are perfectly normal, and need not be worried about. You can still perform perfectly well in an exam with faster pulse, faster breathing, some sweating, a feeling of anxiety and a mildly churning stomach. These symptoms are very unlikely to damage your health, as an exam is quite a small amount of time, and your responses to stress over such a time is hardly going to lead you to chronic (long-term) symptoms. It's when stress gets out of hand that it can become a problem. The symptoms of out-of-control stress often take the form of one or more of the following:

- feelings of panic;
- mind going blank;
- feelings of claustrophobia;
- worry that you're so stressed out you're going to pass out;
- actual nausea;
- abject fear of failure.

Then there's the worrying about worrying! This can include:

- fear that you'll get feelings of panic;
- fear that your mind may go blank;
- fear that feelings of claustrophobia will come over you;
- fear that you'll worry so much that you'll pass out;
- fear that you're going to suffer from real nausea;
- fear that abject fear of failure will result in just that!

All of these symptoms of stress (and stress about the possibility of becoming stressed) can be eased. All are reduced or eliminated by one or more of the following:

- simply getting on and writing what you know is a good answer;
- the feeling that you're making steady progress, and are clocking up marks at a good rate;
- the knowledge that you are being systematic, and tackling the exam in a planned, logical way;
- stopping now and then, giving your brain a minute's rest and thinking about something entirely different and pleasant;
- taking a deeper, slower breath now and then, and allowing your body to relax;

- spending a few minutes getting those things that you're frightened you may forget down onto paper, in essay plans or short lists of essential information, so that you no longer worry about losing them;
- regarding the exam as a game, where you're exercising all of your intelligence to gain as many as possible of the available marks in the time you've got;
- reminding yourself that you don't have to be perfect, and all you have to do is your best, in the time available, with the questions in front of you, and that everyone could do better if they could do it all over again with hindsight;
- reminding yourself that it's only an exam – it's not a life-and-death situation, and that it's unknown for candidates to become seriously injured, or to die, during a final-year exam!

For most of the symptoms of stress, a combination of one or more of the tactics listed above will amount to a robust strategy for eliminating any major impact of the symptoms on your actual performance during the exam. In fact, being a bit stressed normally aids people's performance. There's some extra adrenalin in your system. You think faster. You may well think deeper too.

It's worth exploring in a little more detail that dread of many candidates – having a mental blank. This sounds frightening, and indeed feels frightening when it happens. But it isn't really a 'mental blank' at all. It is better regarded as a temporary loss of function; a temporary power-cut between your brain and your pen. Mental blanks can be avoided. The causes are quite identifiable, and include:

- desperately trying to remember something important that has slipped your conscious mind – something that you really need for the next part of your answer to the question you're working on at the moment (a computer analogy is not remembering which folder a file is in, and forgetting that you can search for it);
- trying to think about all of your answers to all of the exam questions at the same time, and trying to keep all of this at the front of your mind, in case you should forget any of it (a computer analogy is overloading your available memory).

The short answer to both of these causes is 'stop doing it!'. If you're struggling to remember something, and it's not coming back to you, don't struggle any longer. The harder you struggle, the more likely it is that the more damaging symptoms of stress could take over. This is when it is *sensible* to exercise flexibility regarding your timetabled plans for the exam. It is now *sensible* to leave the question you're working on, and move on to a different question – an easier one, or an easier *part* of a different question. Give your brain a rest, and do something straightforward for a while. In the vast majority of cases, after you've been spending some time with a straightforward part of your answers to another question (and clocking up marks in the process), the information you'd been struggling for will filter back into your conscious mind, and you can then, in your own time, go back to the original question and get on with scoring more marks for that too.

Trying to keep all of the information you need at the front of your mind is not a good idea. The best thing to do is to get it down, in note form, onto paper, and then you don't need to worry about keeping it in your mind. Making essay plans is a good way of clearing your brain of the wealth of information that you need to work up, in due course, when you write out your answers to essay-type questions. Writing key formulae down is a good way of avoiding the worry of forgetting them later (but don't go too far the other way, and write down all the formulae that you know, or all those that you might conceivably need in any exam on the topic – only write down those that you *know* you will need to answer the questions you've already decided to attempt).

▶ Getting the marks you deserve – and quite a few extra marks!

Not surprisingly, most of the marks you can score in any exam are for answers to the exam questions, as asked! There aren't many spare marks floating around. Putting down material that *isn't* asked for in the questions is not a good idea, because:

- there won't be marks in the marking scheme for the exam for material that isn't directly needed in response to the questions;
- reading extra, unwanted material actually annoys examiners, as it is essentially a waste of their time, but they still have to read it and check it and work out whether it deserves any credit;
- every minute you spend putting down material that *doesn't* earn you any marks is one minute less to write something that *will* earn you some marks.

Even at the end of the exam, when you've done all you can with the questions, you should take care not to continue writing less-relevant ideas into your answers. You may, however, want to show the examiner that you know more about the question than is actually asked for. In such cases, it's worth making your extra knowledge show as something *additional*, rather than weaving it into your main answers. A subheading along the lines of 'further thoughts on . . .' or 'additional discussion of . . .' can make it clear that this extra material is seen by *you* as going beyond the question. This tends to please examiners much more than when additional material is simply mixed with mainstream answers.

How else can you please examiners?

- **It helps if your writing is relatively easy to read.** That's not the same as your pages simply looking neat, however. Some people's writing looks very neat until you try to actually read it. If your handwriting is really bad (like mine), the best way to try to be readable is to write a little more slowly than you may otherwise have done. Write a little less, but write it more clearly. Try not to write at the speed at which you think – no one can. In final-year examinations, the last thing that should count against anyone is their handwriting, but it still can. Obviously, if there are parts of your answers that the examiner simply can't decipher, you can't be awarded any credit for those parts. Don't apologize on your script for your handwriting! Some candidates do this, but it normally only annoys the examiner further, as bad handwriting is not hard to detect.

- **It helps if it's easy to find where your questions begin and end.** Don't start an answer to a new question halfway down a page. Examiners often mark all the 'Question ones', then all the 'Question twos' and so on, and it is irritating for them to have to search too hard for where your answers to a given question actually start. End your questions clearly too. Rule a line beneath where you've finished your answer. This shows the examiner that you *have* actually finished, and that you haven't simply run out of ideas and moved on to something else. The point at which you end your answer is also the point on your script at which the examiner will enter your mark for the question – you don't want to stop this from happening!

- **In essay-type answers, remind the examiner that you're answering the question.** Don't write out the question of course, but do include in the first sentence of each paragraph something that shows how the paragraph relates to the question as asked. If you can't think of anything, it could mean you're no longer answering the question.

- **In problem-solving questions, show the examiner what you're doing.** It's tempting to just get straight on and solve the problem, and if you do so correctly you may still get full marks. It's when you *don't* reach the correct solution that explaining what you're doing really pays dividends. Examiners are expected to give you credit for everything that *is* correct in your solution to a problem, even if you end up with the wrong answer. It only takes a minute or two more to jot down what you've done for each step along the way to your solution.

- **List any assumptions you find yourself making.** Ideally, you shouldn't have to make any assumptions, but there are times when it becomes inevitable. Sometimes you may need to decide for yourself what the question is *really* asking for. In such cases, it can be worth making this clear to the examiner. Sometimes there could be some data or information missing from the question. One possibility is to ask an invigilator to search out the lecturer who set the question, and find out whether there should have been some further information, but usually this is not your best course of action, because it takes time. It is better to carry on with your answer, stating what you are going to have to assume to continue it.

- *Show* **that you've revisited your answers, and edited and improved them.** Show this neatly! It's tempting to squeeze in second thoughts between your paragraphs, or in the margins, but this looks messy, and it can be difficult to get all you want to say in the small spaces available. When you know you'll need more space than you've got, add a paragraph somewhere else in your script, with *very* clear notes about where the examiner should look for it. Use tactics such as 'Please see Note A on page five', and then on page five, 'Note A from Question one on page three' above your addition. Although it is quite irritating for examiners to have to turn pages backwards and forwards, it is better to gain these extra marks than to lose them. If you've done all you reasonably can to make it straightforward for the examiner, you'll be given credit accordingly.
- *If* **you run out of time during your last answer (or during your last bit of editing), continue in note form.** It is best, of course, not to be seen to have run out of time. When this happens, however, it is better to write a few bullet points to indicate how you would have completed your answer than just to stop midstream. And whatever else, only do this *once* in any exam. If you're seen to do this more than once, the immediate impression is that you're hedging your bets, not thinking fast enough, and trying to get credit for unfinished thinking.

▶ **Making the most of your time between exams**

Don't work all the time! It's tempting to say to yourself, weeks before your exams, 'Oh, I can afford not to do too much preparation for the Friday exam on "Applied Wompology" as I've got nothing between the Monday exam on "Theoretical Carpetbagging" and then. Three days between the exams should cover most of what I need as far as final revision is concerned'. But what about those three days?

- Your head will still be full of Theoretical Carpetbagging at the start.
- You'll be tired, and in need of a rest or a change, not a total immersion in Wompology cramming.
- You'll be only too aware on Tuesday than there's not much time at all until Friday, and your efficiency at revision will be far from its best.

Time between exams is for consolidation, not full-scale revision. It should be *gentle* consolidation. The time you really need your full complement of stamina and energy is *during* each exam, not in the days or hours immediately preceding it. That should seem like a good enough rationale for making sure that you're not going to be in the position of having to do any serious cramming during those days between exams.

What else *shouldn't* you do between exams? A port-mortem on the last one! Doing a post-mortem won't earn you a single additional mark. It may or may not comfort you about the previous exam. It's more likely to discomfort you in fact. The things that will stay in your mind are all those points made by other candidates in their answers which you *didn't* make in your own answers. A post-mortem will deepen your understanding of the topic areas relating to that previous exam, but unless you're going to be measured *again* on these areas, it's much better to work (gently) with the material for your forthcoming exam. This isn't the time to learn any new material for this exam; it's far better to consolidate what you've already learned, and to get in a little more practice at answering questions of the sort you're expecting in the exam.

It's also useful to take some well-deserved rest between exams. You'll do all the better in your next exam if you've regained your mental stamina, and can address the questions well. And whatever you do, don't stay up into the early hours on the day of any exam, revising for it. That could indeed lead to you going into the exam knowing a lot about it, but without the energy to *communicate* your knowledge well in your answers.

What if you find that you can't switch off? There's no point making yourself miserable by escaping from your studies if your conscience is giving you a bad time about it. If this is likely to be your situation, the best strategy is to *prepare* to work gently. Prepare in advance some really concise summary notes of the most important ideas that you will need for the next exam. Then during the time between exams, work only with your summaries of the really important basics, and try not to look at all at your original source materials. A good reason for avoiding your original lecture notes, books and articles is that if you were to re-read them just before the exam, there's every chance that you would only then find in them things that you hadn't yet noticed. This leads you to wonder how much else you haven't yet got to grips with, and leads to a downward 'morale spiral'.

▶ Preparing for the possibility of a viva

After your last exam, it may not all be quite over. You may have a viva. This is an oral exam, where you could be interviewed by one or two of your internal examiners, plus an external one. Sounds scary! Why have vivas, on top of all of your other exams? Some of the reasons why vivas are conducted are:

- They can be part of your university's quality assurance procedures, for the external examiner to see a range of candidates so that comments can be passed back to the university about the general standard of courses and candidates.
- They are often used to interview borderline candidates – more particularly candidates who have fallen just *below* a borderline. An oral examination can give them a chance to show that they're actually better than indicated by their written papers, and they can be moved up over the borderline if they give a good account of themselves at the viva.
- They are also used to establish that the borderlines are in the right places. This means that some candidates who are *not* on a borderline are also interviewed, for reference.

It is usual for *all* candidates to be required to make themselves available, at a given date, place and time, for the possibility that they will be examined by viva. This means that you may be left in doubt regarding the final outcome, whether you feel you've done really well, adequately, or quite badly in your exams. If you find you're actually called for viva on the day, you might well wonder whether you're on a borderline regarding degree classification, or even a pass/fail borderline. It is equally probable that you're not on any borderline, but are one of the candidates providing a reference position to help the examining team give consideration to those candidates who are on borderlines. In other words, it's not worth even worrying about whether or not you're on a borderline. The main thing to remember is that a viva can move you up, if anything.

What types of question could they ask me?

This is a tricky question. The questions *could* be on anything at all relating to your final year. The agenda is, however, likely to be quite specific, depending on the expertise of the external examiner among other things. So does this mean that before your viva you need to revise *all* of the material that you covered for your final year exams, *and* the principal content of any longer pieces of coursework, such as your research project report or dissertation? The short answer is yes!

Let's play detective, and try to narrow the choice down. What *evidence* will the team of examiners have before them (besides you, of course)? The principal evidence will be your results – for everything. The panel of examiners will have before them:

- a printout of all your examination results;
- your coursework records for everything important in your final year (and maybe for previous years too);
- possibly your dissertation or research report, or some other substantial piece of evidence of your overall performance.

The purposes of the team of examiners could include any of the following (and there's no way of telling in advance which of these purposes are specific to your case):

- to decide whether one or more of your exam results is not doing you justice;
- to give you an opportunity to make up for some particular element of your assessment, where your written work showed a problem, or where there was some doubt about how many marks to award you;
- to explore a discrepancy between your coursework and your exam performance – for example, an instance where you seemed to let yourself down unexpectedly in an exam, or where your exam performance was far better than expected from your coursework record;
- to check that something that you did really well in an exam was not just a fluke, by ensuring that you really understand it as well as you seemed to show in that exam;
- to question you about your dissertation or research report, to make sure that it was *you* who did it;
- to give you the chance to show that you are actually rather better than your records indicate, and are worth moving up over a borderline;
- or simply to use you as a reference candidate, to decide whether other candidates deserve moving up into the same category of award as you have already achieved.

This narrows down your agenda considerably. Some of the main areas for pre-viva revision boil down to:

- **Polish up areas where *you* know your exam performance let you down.** This *is* the time to indulge in some strategic, well-focused post-mortem activity. Look back over your exams, and identify questions where you know you floundered. Your viva may give you another chance to show that you could have done better with one or more of these questions.
- **Polish up your strengths too.** The examiners may want to check that you are really as good as some of your best answers indicated. Alternatively, they may simply want to put you at ease by asking you some questions about areas where you did well. In either case, it's important that your best performances aren't indicated, by your viva answers, to have been flukes!

- **Read back through your dissertation or research project.** Look at it in a different way: if *you* were reading it now as an examiner, what questions would you ask the candidate about it? What were the best bits? What were your most interesting findings or conclusions? How would you check that the candidate really understood what has been written? How would you check that the candidate had actually done the work? What were the weaker parts, and how would you check that the candidate could do better than was indicated by what was written? What feedback have you already had on your work, and have you taken on board any suggestions for further development or improvement of your work?

The three areas described above are your principal preparation agenda for the possibility of having a viva. Remember it is still only a possibility, but that it's one that is well worth being prepared for. It is worth spending about half of your time on this agenda, and using the other half of your time to remind yourself of the main things you learned for your final exams. It's also a good idea to get in some practice at doing vivas.

How can you practise for a viva?

An oral exam measures some different things about you. It measures how well you answer questions on the spot, questions posed by people who are experts. It measures how well you can talk about your subject knowledge, and communicate it to other people. It gives an indication of how quickly you can think. It measures how clearly you can express yourself in speech. It measures how well you can cope with unexpected questions. It can show whether you're the sort of person who tries to bluff your way through when there is something that you don't understand. It can show whether you've actually got a better (or worse!) grasp of your subject matter than was indicated by your written exam performance and written coursework

A key element of a wise strategy for preparing for written exams is to practise answering exam questions in writing. In the same way, for your viva you need to practise *speaking* answers to questions. Who can ask you such questions? The best people are your fellow students, preparing for the same possibility. It's best to throw away all thoughts now of competing with your fellow students, and concentrate on helping each other to put on a good show at vivas. Students often spend the last few days before a viva quizzing each other, and role-playing examiners. This can be enjoyable as well as productive.

▶ Post-exam blues: where did those years go?

You may find it hard to believe that you could have post-exam blues after your final-year exams are over! You may, however, already know what post-exam blues feel like. There's a sense of anticlimax. You've been keyed up for what seems for ever, and then, quite suddenly, it's all over. The moment when it *really* feels all over is after your viva (or after the viva you prepared for, but didn't actually have). This time, it is in fact all over. At least your final year is past. You may never have a formal exam again. You certainly won't have such a batch of crucial exams again, unless of course you decide to do another degree later in your life. You may well have *important* exams in future, such as a viva for a masters degree or doctorate, but that's not the same – it's much more specific and focused for a start. The agenda may be deeper, but is much narrower.

The end of your final year is a turning point. The next part of your life will be different. It may be entirely different, in a new place, with a new job, new friends and new challenges. Or it may be in the same familiar surroundings, but this time as a research student, with a new and different status. Or it may be as a researcher at a different institution.

Preparing for, and undertaking your final exams has stresses, but finishing them also brings its own kind of stress. Change is a cause of stress. One of the principal elements of change after your exams is being able to call your time your own, perhaps for the first time in months. There's still some stress while you're waiting for the final results, but however hard you worry about them it won't change them now.

Post-exam blues take many forms. Some people become irritable and unsettled. Others get small things out of perspective, and even become downright neurotic for a while. Relationships can suffer. For ages you may have been wanting more time to give to a relationship, and now you've got it what on earth do you do with it? Your partner may have been desperate to spend more time with you, but can the pair of you cope with having too much time to spend together?

You may have been putting off starting your real job hunting until now, and now you've got the time, have you the faintest idea where to start? You may just want to sleep, and sleep – not an unnatural response to being tired, exhilarated, and with the pressure quite suddenly off.

You might fall into the trap of 'if only' thinking. Now that it's all over, if only you'd worked harder, if only you'd attempted Question five instead of Question seven on that penultimate paper, if only you hadn't eaten that huge curry before your viva and had felt better on the day, and so on. Don't look back, other than to learn useful lessons for your own future. Don't waste your energy on the 'if only' dimension.

You may have been yearning for all the pressure to be off. And now it is. But what is this world without pressure you've been anticipating? And this strange new pressure of not having any pressure on you? Can you cope without having a fixed agenda?

How about a holiday? How about a year off? Post-exam blues don't last for very long. Soon you'll feel that it was a long time since you were revising and writing exam answers. You may well continue, for years, to revisit exams in dreams (or is it nightmares?) and wake up to the relief that you haven't got any more such exams.

The best remedies for post-exam blues include:

- keeping busy (maybe diverting your energies into job hunting, if you've not already sorted that out);
- company, both people in the same position as you, and others who know nothing about final years;
- getting back to fitness, returning to sports and exercise patterns that you may have abandoned during that final year;
- getting back into hobbies that you may have had to give up for what seems like ages;
- relaxing, as and when you can – winding down.

Uncomfortable as post-exam blues can feel, they're not a serious complaint. They're hardly likely to be fatal. Like a cold, they run their course, then go. Like a cold, the remedies relieve the symptoms, and allow the time to pass more comfortably until you're out of it.

Leaving the institution you've got to know

There is naturally some grief. It's almost like bereavement. There is also, of course, a lot of excitement. Leaving the place where you've been for years can be hard. There may have been many times when you couldn't wait to get out of the place, but now that you *can* go, it suddenly seems more attractive, more reassuring, more comfortable. And there's the matter of parting with most of the people who have been part of your life for a significant while. It suddenly can feel lonely out there in the rest of the world. There's the excitement of moving on in your life, but there's also the pain of not being able to return to what was your life in your final year.

Things have changed. *You* have changed – not least, you're now a graduate. You've got letters after your name. You've grown up academically. People expect different things of you. In the overall picture of your life, you're still in a period of very rapid change. Graduates who've been out in the world of commerce and industry for three years change at least as much as you did in your years at university. Even postgraduates who stay at university continue to change, if not so rapidly. Keep asking yourself two questions: 'What can the university still do for me now?' and 'What can I, if I choose, still do for the university?'.

This final leaving is not so final! Most graduates stay in touch with at least some of their friends from student days, often for years and years. People have been known to travel back from the other side of the world for a 25-year reunion event. Many graduates maintain contact with the institution too, and join in with alumni events. The pain of leaving soon becomes dissipated by the challenges and exhilaration of moving into the next stages of your life and career. Don't cut ties with your university after you've left it. Find reasons to go back and visit. There will still be people there that you know. At least one of your referees will still work there. At least some of your friends will still be studying there. And the library is still there. That contains all manner of things which may be useful to you for the next stage of your life. Now you've got time to explore not just the well-trodden aisles relating to your subject area, but anything else that interests you. When you go back as a graduate, lecturers will look at you differently. You're closer to being one of them now – you're not just another student.

 Personal action plan

Which do you think is your wisest existing exam technique?

Jot down any additional ideas of your own for improving your performance in time-constrained, unseen written exams:

What's the *worst* tactic you ever used in an exam? (Don't forget it!):

What's your own best strategy for calming yourself down if ever you feel tense in exams?

What particular actions are *you* going to take at the end of your exams to squeeze those extra marks out of your examiners?

Have you any good tips for pleasing examiners, and earning more 'benefit of the doubt' marks at the same time?

What are you now going to do between your final exams?

How are you going to prepare wisely for a viva?

Have you had post-exam blues before now, and if so, did you find any good cures? (Write to me, c/o Open University Press, and I'll include them, duly acknowledged, of course, in the next edition of this book.):

6 Thinking about research and higher degrees

▶ Is this really your final year?

For many students, the final year does not turn out to be a final year! They continue to do one or more higher degrees. Some have planned this all along, and have tuned in their final year towards opening up opportunities for research and further study. For others, it's a sudden inspiration. They'd planned to get a job, but along comes an opportunity to stay a student for a bit longer. Some even turn down well-paid jobs they've secured, and opt for the life of a research student, hoping that this will lead them in due course to an even better life.

This chapter is only to start you thinking about research. For much more detail about how to prepare yourself for life as a postgraduate student, and for the possibility of heading for a career as an academic, other Open University Press study guides will give you a wealth of further information and guidance. *The Good Research Guide* by Martyn Denscombe (1998) is written primarily for graduates in social science areas, but has a lot of suggestions which apply to any kind of research. *How to Research* by Lorraine Blaxter, Christina Hughes and Malcolm Tight (1996) covers research in all sorts of different areas, and contains references to a wide range of further reading on research. In particular, *How to Research* helps you to get a grip on your own research *thinking*. *How to Get a PhD* by Estelle Phillips and D. S. Pugh (2000, third edition) is regarded as a bible for PhD students. *Doing your Research Project* by Judith Bell (1999, third edition) focuses on research in education and social science, and gives a wealth of advice about planning, structuring and implementing research. *The Research Student's Guide to Success* by Pat Cryer (1996) brings a wealth of experience to help you do everything from applying to become a research student to getting your higher degree, whatever your discipline. With all of this specialist, focused information available to you in books such as those mentioned above, I would just like to help you to think, in the context of *your* final year, whether this is a direction in which you might like to head, or whether you may still prefer to keep your options open, and consider looking for your first postgraduate job as well as keeping an eye open for research prospects.

▶ Becoming a postgraduate student

If you've already decided to continue at university after your degree, or if you're just weighing up the pros and cons of making such a decision, it's worth looking at what's different about being a postgraduate student. There are several significant differences; only some are listed below.

- You're now on the other side of the fence. You're an academic – albeit a fairly junior and inexperienced one.
- You *may* be not quite so hard up!
- You may be no longer part of a class or cohort, and may be much more in control of your own study, with a much higher level of responsibility for maintaining your studying.
- You may feel quite lonely, at least at first, especially if you're researching more or less on your own.
- You may still be part of a class, on a 'taught' masters or even 'taught' doctorate programme, but the curriculum will be much more specialized, narrower and deeper.
- You may have a much closer relationship with one or two relatively senior academics (your research supervisors) and may feel light years away from their level of experience and expertise.
- You may have supervisors who are on your tail and keep you under close supervision, and expect a lot of you, and say so.
- The library will seem a different place altogether, as you get to know intimately the stock of books and journals in your research area, and as you find out much more about how to borrow from other sources.
- You may have a desk, or a share of one, somewhere *in* the university (and if you're lucky a drawer in a filing cabinet) and work there rather than in your own space at home.
- You may have a corner in a laboratory, with your own equipment and your own coffee mug!
- You could have relatively distant supervisors, who leave most of it up to you, and are quite hard to find and talk to.
- You may find yourself spending some of your time *doing* things on the other side of the fence: teaching, running the odd tutorial, demonstrating in an undergraduate laboratory and even giving your first lectures.

These things are typical of some of the differences between being a postgraduate student and an undergraduate. You may have tasted some of these already, while doing a research project or dissertation for your first degree, but then it was only *part* of your overall picture – as a researcher it will be the *whole* picture. As an undergraduate, the end was firmly in sight (if not always in mind). As a postgraduate, the end may be somewhat less determined. There's more chance of slipping by the wayside without anyone noticing! In fact, that's the biggest danger. Postgraduate failures are rarely actual failures – most of them are 'non-completions'. And there's more time between vacations – what vacations?

What, no vacations?

If you've already been on campus, for whatever reason, during the student vacations, you will have noticed that there are still people around. Many lecturers do most of their research when students are away. And postgraduate students are there too. That's when their supervisors have more time to see them and work with them. That's when the library is less crowded, and the community of academics and researchers can get on with their reading and writing.

For most postgraduates, there aren't 'vacations' at all. They may take a holiday from time to time, but then it's likely to be a couple of weeks or at most a month. Some hardly take any time off. And the working hours are different from those of undergraduates. Some postgraduates arrive on campus just about as soon as they can get into the library or into the buildings they're working in. They may even have keys of their own. Many postgraduates are there well into the evening, and may only leave their buildings when they're closed for the night – if they close at all. If you're working with several other research students, for example in a laboratory, you may need to take turns using equipment and facilities, and stagger your working hours to match availability.

There may still be lectures you're required or expected to attend. But the rest of your timetable will be of your own making. You're unlikely to be advised to go away and spend less time studying! Your research supervisors may be conscientious academics, working every available hour on doing their own research and writing it up for publication, and going away to conferences and symposia to present their findings to the rest of the research community in your discipline. Their life may be dominated by pressure to get their work published, and to secure research funding for themselves and for their research students.

All in all, the time factor is completely turned around from being an undergraduate. This will mean pacing yourself in a different way. You need a different kind of stamina as a postgraduate. You need staying power. You need to be able to persist at things. There may be days, or even months, when nothing actually goes right in your research. You may spend ages planning an element of research, and it simply turns out not to lead to anything. Then there will be days when everything seems to be forging ahead, and you hardly dare stop while the going is good. And what about the rest of your life now?

Can you afford this?

Some postgraduates are even poorer than undergraduate students. They may be paying their own fees, and living on whatever they can put together from part-time work, occasional teaching duties and so on. Others are on a research grant of one kind or another. At first, this can seem quite generous compared to finance as an undergraduate – until you remember that it's not just to keep you going for a limited number of weeks spanning a term or semester, but for most of the weeks in the year. Your expectations of life may have changed quite a lot since getting your first degree. You may have family responsibilities to cope with. You may now be running a car.

Funding for research is almost always relatively short term. You may have a short-term contract. You may have to reapply to get your funding renewed every year. There may be a set time within which you've got to get your higher degree, and if you haven't done it by the end of this time, there may be no further financial support at all for you, and you could end up having to get a job *and* finish off your masters or doctorate thesis at the same time. This is hard! And in any case there will be a regulations deadline after which you simply will not be allowed to submit for your higher degree. Many sad stories relate to candidates caught between job pressures and an unmet deadline.

At almost any time, it would be financially attractive to give up being a postgraduate student, and go for a job. The difference could be a doubled or trebled income – and a great deal less work. Why is research so poorly paid? How do postgraduates ever manage to get higher degrees? Think about the following before you embark on working towards a higher degree:

- a higher degree may enhance your salary and prospects for the rest of your career;
- you may have a wider choice of job opportunities with a higher degree, and therefore more chance of finding something that you will really enjoy doing;
- you may want to prove to yourself that you can do more than get a first degree;
- you may be driven to prove to other people that you can do it;
- many research students are motivated by *wanting* to have a higher degree – for example looking forward to being addressed as 'Dr so-and-so' rather than 'Ms so-and-so'.

There's more to it, of course, than money, position and pride. There's a great deal of satisfaction attached to successfully researching a topic, publishing your results and feeling that you're making a contribution to pushing back the frontiers in a discipline area, however specialized. There is satisfaction in belonging to an élite 'club' of people who share detailed knowledge of a specialized subject area. These are the things that keep postgraduates going when the going is tough.

To help you to clarify your own driving forces towards postgraduate study it could be useful to return to the 'diamond-9' exercise (see Introduction), and do it again, this time widening your horizons to take on board the possibilities that would be opened up to you by a higher degree. Postgraduate students really need motivation. Most have lots of it – those who don't have enough soon leave!

Are you up to it?

Quite a few graduates wonder whether or not they're up to postgraduate study or research. There are many casualties. There's less chance of failure, but more of non-completion. Most postgraduates feel quite anxious about whether or not they've got what it takes, especially at the start of their work towards a higher degree. Some prefer to test the waters by taking up positions as research assistants, which are not dependent upon them registering at the outset for a higher degree. The main difference for them is that their responsibility is helping other people with their research, rather than getting down to some of their own.

Your final year will have given you several indications of whether you're up to postgraduate study. These include:

- the level to which your research project succeeded, and how competent you found yourself to be at taking responsibility for your own work on your project;
- the extent to which you succeeded to write up your work in a dissertation or major report, and picked up relevant skills for writing up larger amounts of work;
- comments from project supervisors, who may have advised you that you've got what it takes to go on to a higher degree;
- comparisons you made between yourself and other people you encountered who were already doing postgraduate study.

In the final analysis, however, it seems that most people who really *want* to get a higher degree, and who are prepared to put in what is needed to get one, do get one. It is not surprising that the most common doctorate is one in 'philosophy'. It doesn't much matter what the actual subject is, it's the philosophy that gets one there!

▶ Choosing a topic

There are no hard and fast rules for how to go about this. The only certainty is that it's more complex than it may have been as an undergraduate, where you may have been presented with a list of likely project topics, and asked to negotiate your own selection. The range of possibilities for postgraduate topic identification ranges widely, with the extremes being:

- talking to one or more academics who may be looking for research students, and finding out on which areas of their research they would suggest you might work with (or for) them;
- thinking of a topic of your own, and approaching likely supervisors to see if you can find someone who will support your case.

If you're registering for a higher degree, there will be hurdles to overcome. Your research proposal will need to be approved by an appropriate committee (for example a 'research degrees committee'), and your proposed supervisor(s) will need to be approved to be sufficiently qualified or experienced to oversee your work. Decisions may need to be made as to whether your research proposal is appropriate for a masters degree or for a doctorate, or whether there will be a time (say the end of your first postgraduate year) when you will be advised (or told) which of these options remain open to you.

Probably the best advice you can be given about choosing your topic is to keep your options as open as you can. In other words, make your research proposal broad enough, and flexible enough, to allow you to continue to interpret it as your work proceeds. Don't put all of your eggs into one basket if you can avoid doing so. The nature of research is that sometimes what you are looking for turns out to be not nearly so interesting or important as something that crops up along the way. If you've got the flexibility to retune your work towards what is interesting and important, you're at a distinct advantage. Ideally, a research proposal should be tight enough to appear to be a strong case for the research degrees committee stage, but slack enough to allow you to follow up interesting leads without coming into conflict with your registered application for a higher degree.

▶ Choosing a supervisor

If your first degree, and particularly your final year, was phenomenally successfully, you could have a queue of prospective research supervisors wanting you to work with them! If, at the other end of the scale, you're struggling to gain entry to postgraduate work, you may be in the position of trying hard to make yourself a sufficiently attractive proposition to gain just one human being prepared (and able) to be your supervisor. In either case, it's worth thinking about what sort of person will be a successful supervisor for you. Choosing a supervisor is *your* decision at the end of the day. You might not have much choice! The following list of questions may help you to make your decision, and to take on the respective strengths and limitations of the different kinds of people who supervise research.

Types of research supervisor

Sally Brown, in an article in *The Times Higher* in 1998 typified many of the problems that can arise from the nature and availability of research supervisors. Though humorous, her categories are well-known in universities!

- **'Lone Ranger and Tonto'**. 'You noble but lesser mortal, me great hero. I will give you access to language and interpret for you. You follow my guidance exactly and I'll get you through OK.' This sort of supervisor may bring a measure of safety to your research, and may lead you towards fame yourself, but what happens when you outgrow following guidance exactly? That could be the end of the road for your relationship with such a supervisor, who may then turn quite hostile.
- **'Florence Nightingale'**. Illuminating, leads the way, silent strength, unobtrusive, remote, cool. Sounds good? But do *you* need someone who's unobtrusive, with silent strength? Maybe you need someone a bit more pushy to keep you on track?
- **'Red Queen and Alice'**. Capricious, autocratic, unreliable, ultimately dangerous. Such a supervisor can be great fun, of course. If you are very confident and buoyant, you may find such a supervisor quite stimulating. But if not?!
- **'Mummy knows best'**. Nurturing, warm, kind, highly controlling, on at you all the time. You might have left home to escape from this kind of supervisor once already! Or you might be missing her? The 'nurturing, warm and kind' is fine, of course. It's the 'highly controlling, on at you all the time' bit that can become a problem, especially over an extended timespan.
- **'Lord Lucan'**. Just not there for you! You wouldn't *knowingly* choose a research supervisor who was going to be hard to find, but some people end up with one! You need to check out that your intended supervisor does actually exist, in a real place, often enough for your needs.
- **'Major Tom to ground control'**. Distant, communicating only electronically, a voice from the ether, out of control. This sort of supervisor is no use to you whatsoever if you're the sort of postgraduate student who

needs to see a face to talk to. However, a combination of electronic availability with face-to-face meetings can be ideal, as electronic communication can often be far faster than arranging a meeting, if you want a quick suggestion or comment from your supervisor.

- **'The Godfather'.** 'You give me respect and follow my autocratic directions, and I'll protect you.' There are plenty of examples of this sort of supervisor around. The autocratic directions might well pave a safe way to postgraduate success – ask some other research students supervised by this kind of person. However, some 'Godfathers' are heretics, and can lead you firmly to obscurity.
- **'The obscurantist'.** You lose the plot the minute you leave the room after talking to this one. There may be an element of this picture in any supervisor–student relationship at postgraduate level. During your degree studies, discussions with tutors tended to be focused around the syllabus – relatively well-trodden ground. The first time you talk to the same people about their research specialism, you often find that they are talking in a much harder language. It can still work though. A well-managed meeting with an 'obscurantist' is one where the pair of you jot down notes for you to take away, sufficient to allow you to revisit the encounter, in slower motion, after the event.
- **'The White Rabbit'.** Always in a rush, under pressure, 'Leave me alone, I'm late'. A dangerous species! As a research student, there will be occasions where you really do need some unhurried time with your supervisor. Lack of such time at crucial stages can cause your research to drift off target.
- **'Stranger on the road to Emmaus'.** Only present when needed, unobtrusive, all-knowing, supportive. This may sound ideal, but will *you* be able to justify and keep this supervisor's respect too?

Which would *you* choose? You choice probably tells you as much about yourself as about the sort of research supervisor who will work for you. The nature of the research supervisor–research student relationship is quite different in some respects to anything you may have experienced before.

Dangers with supervisors

Some of the main problem areas are:

- **Falling out.** As an undergraduate it didn't matter too much if you fell out with one particular member of staff, but as a research student if you fall out with your research supervisor it's big trouble for you!
- **Getting too close!** This is just as dangerous as falling out, for different reasons. An experienced and successful research supervisor knows

where to draw the boundaries between comradeship and friendship, and your successful development.

- **Perceived favouritism.** This can be a problem if you're one of several research students working for one supervisor. Life isn't always equitable, and you may be the new person in the team, and feel that others are getting all the help *they* need, at your expense.
- **Illness, absence, unavailability.** Many research students suffer from these supervisor conditions. These, of course, are quite out of your control. Your preliminary research into who's likely to turn out to be a successful supervisor for you may throw some light on their track record in these respects.

It's also worth thinking about ethics and integrity issues, particularly those of ownership and *authorship* of the publications that should arise in due course from your research. There are three principal possibilities:

- **Supervisors who will use your work primarily for *their* benefit.** This category includes supervisors who make very little contribution to your work, but get their names on your publications. This may be forgivable if it's entirely due to them that you got the chance (and perhaps the funding) to undertake the research in the first place.
- **Supervisors who use your work for *your* benefit.** This may seem an attractive proposition at first sight, but it may not be the strongest of driving forces and the supervision you get may not be as robust as when supervisors themselves also benefit from your work.
- **Supervisors who use your work for mutual benefit.** If they are as keen to make sure your work succeeds as you are, you can see that there is a stronger driving force for them to make a good job of supervising you.

Factors to consider when selecting your supervisor

How can you make an informed decision about choosing yourself an ideal research supervisor? The following checklist of questions (and explanations) may help you to decide what's going to work out for you.

Have they already supervised successfully?

Supervising research, like anything else, involves skills which need to be practised and developed. Someone who has already supervised one or more higher degree students to successful completion is obviously a better bet for you as a potential supervisor than someone who has not yet done this. Someone whose previous research students have dropped out is a risky option. That said, there's got to be a first time to be a research supervisor, and it is worth considering as a supervisor someone who has not done it before, if they've got other good things going for them. Look at the other checklist points to help you decide.

What's their publication record like?

You're going to need their help to get into print with the results of your research, perhaps co-publishing with them. If the last time they published was ten years ago, take it as a warning sign. It could indicate that their own research is well past its sell-by date. They may no longer carry any weight in the field. You need someone whose research is respected and who knows which are the best (and worst) journals in the field today, and can advise authoritatively about where to place the findings of your work.

What do their research students have to say about them?

This is well worth investigating. Ask them loaded questions such as 'What's the best thing about Dr Bloggs as your supervisor?' and 'What's the worst thing?' Ask them 'Would you still choose Dr Bloggs if you were starting from scratch again?' Ask further questions such as 'What is most likely to annoy your supervisor?', 'What have you found to be the best way to get the most from your supervisor?' and 'How much guidance are you provided with, and how much is it up to you?'

Do they seem to get on with colleagues in the department?

If you were to become a research student of someone who was already unpopular with other members of staff in the department, you'd be at a disadvantage from the start. If your potential supervisor is well liked (and respected) by colleagues, you'll get your share of reflected cooperation from others in the department.

Are their research ideas realistic?

You don't want your research to turn out to be a wild-goose chase. Nor do you want it to be so straightforward that it's not publishable. You also need to feel confident that what you are going to research is not something that someone else will publish just before you're ready to do so (though there is always some chance of this happening in popular fields). Who can help you decide whether or not a potential supervisor's ideas are realistic? Their own research students will have things to tell you about this, but remember that their views are likely to be loaded in favour of their supervisor's ideas – their future depends on this! Try asking other academics in the department how they rate a potential supervisor's research profile. Try asking other academics in the same field, but in other institutions, what they think.

How do you think you will get on with them?

Whatever else, your relationship with your supervisor will be specific to you. First impressions aren't always to be trusted, but first impressions are far better than no data at all. You can expect, for example, to be able to tell almost immediately if a particular supervisor is just *not* an option for you.

Will they have enough time for me?

Academics who are highly successful are likely to be very busy people. They may travel far and wide, and be difficult to pin down to regular appointments with you. If they're already supervising several different research students, their time for you could be even more limited. Conversely, busy people often do what they do really well, make good use of their time and can help you to make good use of yours.

Will they give me too much rope? Or too little?

You probably know yourself well enough to know what will work for you. Some research students thrive when given a lot of control of their own research, others prefer to have a fairly strict regime, at least until they're successfully under way.

How to alienate your supervisor

Let's look ahead to research in progress. It may be very much in *your* hands how to maintain a good relationship with your research supervisor. Much depends upon what happens when you meet periodically. It's worth looking at some of the things that supervisors like least!

- **Research students just not turning up for meetings**. This alienates supervisors faster than anything else (not surprisingly). Being late is bad enough – it shows disrespect for supervisors' precious time.
- **Students turning up unprepared**. This too is interpreted as a sign of disrespect. Supervisors need to feel that you are valuing their time and energy. If *you* turn up well-prepared, even if *they* haven't done the same, they're more likely to prepare for your next meeting.
- **Students who turn up unprepared, but don't admit it, and try to bluff their way out of the situation**. This tactic is likely to damage any supervisor–student relationship really quickly.
- **Students who seem not to have any ideas of their own, and who regard meetings with their supervisor as 'tell me everything you know about what I'm supposed to be trying to do' occasions**. Supervisors can quickly tire of spoonfeeding research students. A fair amount

of direction may be required at the outset, but it should not take long for research students to start thinking for themselves.

- **Students who turn up very prepared, but completely on the wrong track.** This is even worse! A supervisor is then likely to start to have serious doubts about whether the student is up to the agreed research programme.

▶ To research or not to research?

I hope that this short chapter will have helped you to address this question. If you've already decided to head towards being a postgraduate researcher, I hope you will feel that you know a little more about what you may be letting yourself in for. If you've decided *not* to move towards an academic career, I hope that you now feel you are a little better informed about what you have decided to miss. In the final analysis, it is *your* decision. It is never too late to change your mind either way. There are plenty of successful academics who were on the verge of accepting something entirely different when a research opportunity came up for them, and who took this opportunity, and found that it changed their lives. Whether for better or worse, they often continue to ponder!

 Personal action plan

Have you decided whether or not to go in for research, or are you still keeping your options open?

Jot down ideas you may already have about the fields of study you may wish to research:

What could be *your* main driving forces, to keep you on track if you go into research?

What particular strengths do you think you already have that are relevant to research?

What do you think could be the most serious challenge you may face when starting off as a research student?

What sort of supervisor would you choose if you had a completely free choice?

What will *you* have to do to avoid alienating your supervisor? (You know what your bad habits are likely to be!):

7 Writing your CV and making job applications

▶ Now or later?

The ideal strategy is to make your entire final year dual purpose: aiming for your degree *and* securing your first job after graduation. You might have already decided *not* to try to achieve anything more in your final year than to get your degree safely. If you've made a final decision of this sort, I hope that you will find the last two chapters of this book useful to you later, but I would like you to at least read through the start of this chapter, and check that you are firm in your decision.

Reasons why it is not a good idea to postpone job hunting until after you've got your degree include:

- **You are likely to need to be earning some money as soon as reasonably possible**. You may have loans to pay off. You may have a lifestyle to keep up. After studying for some years, you will want to get on with the rest of your life.
- **You don't want to be seen as *not* having found a job for some time after graduating**. If application forms and your CV show a gap between graduating and seeking employment, some employers may wonder why you weren't successful in finding a job straight after getting your degree. What was wrong with you? Why didn't you get appointed?
- **You need to use your degree well before its 'best-before date'**. This is more serious in some disciplines than in others. In disciplines which are advancing rapidly (computing, for example), next year's graduates will be substantially more up to date than this year's cohort.
- **You want to show potential employers that you can work for your degree *and* apply for jobs at the same time**. Employers need people who can do more than one thing at once. They prefer candidates who are good at multi-tasking. They respect candidates who know where they're aiming for.

An even stronger reason for combining job hunting with your final-year studies is that it gives you time to become *better* at job hunting. Like anything else, job hunting depends on a set of skills that are best honed by practice, trial and error. The longer you practise the better you become at job hunting. The more you find out about job hunting the less time it takes you to put in a sound application – you become more efficient as well as more effective. Being more efficient pays dividends as your final year progresses, and enables you to keep the time and energy you spend on job hunting down, allowing more time for your studies.

▶ Finding and choosing posts to apply for

Use the expertise available to you. Universities have careers services, run by people with a lot of knowledge and experience. They can save you a great deal of time and energy by alerting you to the most likely sources of job advertisements for the sort of job you have in mind. They can broaden your target range by alerting you to other career possibilities which may be open to you, which you may never have thought of on your own. They are likely to have contacts with major employers in your discipline area. They may well arrange for employers to visit the university, and arrange interviews for you without you having to take time away from your studies to travel to distant destinations (time saved in your final year is always useful). They may be able to provide you with a cuttings service of adverts from newspapers, magazines and other publications, so that you don't miss the most relevant opportunities, and saving you yet more time by not having to search out (or buy) the source materials yourself.

You need to work *with* the staff of your careers service, and not expect them to do all of the work for you. You need to spend time helping them to tune in to exactly who you are, what sort of person you are and what your hopes and ambitions are. You need them to feel they are valued by you. They know a lot about the best processes for applying for jobs. They know a lot about application forms, CVs and how to go about interviews.

Employment agencies and temping

Many students gain valuable work-related experience through temping, often arranged through employment agencies. Employment agencies may also give you useful feedback on your job application techniques, and may provide relevant training too. They may indeed help you to track down your first postgraduate full-time appointment, or at least give you further insights into where best to track down likely sources of advertisements for the sort of jobs that you have in mind. Their range and experience may be less specialized than your university careers service, but they may have better contacts in specific employment areas. In your final year, it's always useful to have other people working on your behalf, provided that it does not take too much of *your* time and energy to get them working for you well.

► Using your CV to sell your strengths

What's a CV?

The abbreviation CV stands for 'curriculum vitae' – the story of your life (so far). It's a document that you design about yourself. You can adapt its size, content and structure to suit each individual application which you submit. You can make an executive summary about yourself, aiming for a single, well-structured page, or you can spread it out onto a few more pages to give a full account of your achievements and tell a detailed story of the wonderful, employable candidate that you are.

Your CV should whet its readers' appetites, and aim to make them wish to find out more about you, and shortlist you for interview. By adapting (quickly) your CV to suit the purposes of each individual application you make you can increase its fitness for purpose, so that readers see at once that this is not just a standard document that you send to everyone, and that you are the sort of candidate who takes the time and trouble to furnish a CV which relates directly to the nature of the job you're applying for.

How big should your CV be?

Your CV will grow with your career. By the time you apply for mid-career jobs or promotion opportunities, your CV could be as much as ten pages long. When you're applying for lots of different jobs, however, at the start of your career, you may be able to get all of the key information into as little as a single, full, well-laid-out side of A4, or (more likely) onto between two and four sides of A4. Your CV needs to tell its story quickly and efficiently – if it is too long, readers will get bored and it will lose its impact.

Seven reasons for writing your CV

- Many employers will *ask* you to send one, along with a letter of application and/or a completed application form.

- Most employers *want* to see that you can organize information about yourself in your own way, and put it together in writing (print!) into a coherent, intelligible document.
- If you have a CV ready, you have something to give to, or send to, a prospective employer at any time during your final year, including times when you're far too busy to stop and write one.
- A CV gives you the chance to sell yourself to prospective employers, where *you* are in charge of what you write, and how you tell your story about yourself.
- Once you've written your CV, you can print a few copies off and have them ready for those occasions when otherwise you may not have bothered to follow up a job opportunity.
- You can keep your CV bang up to date on computer disk, so that you don't have to go scrabbling around for details such as grades, dates, jobs you've already done, and so on.
- Your CV can contain just about all the information you're likely to need for each application form, making it much quicker (and less boring) to complete such forms.

Don't stick too closely to any template

There are various standard ways of putting together information in your CV, and the most usual content of CVs tends to fall under common headings, usually presented in roughly the same order. However, if *your* CV looks just like those of all the other applicants it's not going to make your application stand out from the pack. Ideally, in one way or another, your CV should give the message 'Here's someone worth finding out more about'. Many of the completed applications considered by employers may look more or less the same as yours, with candidates having similar qualifications to yours, and broadly comparable background experience. Your CV should look more attractive, and read more interestingly, than others in the pile. It should also be fine-tuned to appear particularly relevant to each job you're applying for.

Ingredients for your CV

Some of the central elements of a CV are listed below, in approximately the order that most people use. As you look at each item in turn, you may like to make a very early draft of your CV if you've not already written one, or check your CV and start polishing and adjusting it if you've already got one.

Who are you?

- **Who are you, and how can we contact you?** This is where you give your name, contact addresses, phone, fax, email, and so on. Not much research to do here. You may also think about whether to give your date of birth – you don't *have* to, of course, but most applicants do, and if you don't, employers could wonder why. You don't *have* to give your gender (if it's not clear from your name) but if you've got a name that could be interpreted as either gender, do you *want* the possibility of employers thinking your gender is the other one? However, there are a few tips which may help you. Make sure it's clear which name is which. If you've got a forename (say Owen) that is also frequently other people's family name, and perhaps a family name that is many other people's forenames, use bold print or capitals for the family name, and normal print for the forename. For example:

  Owen **John** or Owen **JOHN**

  would make it less likely that Owen John was welcomed wrongly at interview with 'Come in, Mr Owen'.
- **You'll need to give your full name somewhere and your CV is the best place.** Some people have been blessed with terrible names. Others have already become known by a familiar name, sometimes related to an original forename, and sometimes quite different! If you're Victoria, you might (or might not) be known as Vikki. Someone called Aloysius Reginald Watson may simply have become known as Reg or even Doc! It can be useful to make this clear through your CV from the start, and put 'CV: Reg Watson' as a running header on all the pages, at the same time as stating the full name at the top of the first page. It can make you feel much more comfortable at interview if people refer to you as you're normally addressed, rather than over-formally.
- **You really do need to be contactable.** Quite often candidates are invited for interview at the last minute, for example if someone else drops out. Try to give one or more address and phone number where you're *sure* that a postal message will get to you within a day and a phone message will get to you within an hour or two. If you are *easily* contacted by fax, include this number. Beware, though: people interpret a fax having got through as meaning it's got through to the right person. Email contact is fine if you read your emails every day, and if the technology works every time (it never does!).
- Your date of birth doesn't change, so (if you're revealing your age) it is better to state this on your CV than to give your age, which changes once a year! The people reading your CV are bright enough to calculate your age if they want it, and you want to give it.

What about you?

- **What are your qualifications?** Your CV is your chance to list these in your own way, including (maybe in brackets) the details of the qualification you're working towards (exact title of the award, which institution will be awarding it and the anticipated date of confirmation that you have gained it, and so on). Normal practice is to include on your CV only relevant information about qualifications. You may or may not want to go into a lot of detail about the grades of all the exams you passed at school, for example.
- **Have you held down a job already?** Employers like to know that besides being a wonderful, well-educated person, you can actually get up in the morning, turn up on time, and get on with other people well enough to keep a job. The jobs you have already done may well just have been part-time ones, and could be quite irrelevant to your career plans, but it's still worth putting some details in your CV. You can decide later *which* job details you'll actually include each time you adapt your CV for a particular application.
- **Are you a nice person?** Of course you are, but you need to *show* it. A few details of the sort of societies, clubs, hobbies, pastimes that make up the rest of your life can be useful evidence that here is a person who's not a social misfit or a recluse. You may well have developed important key skills through your leisure activities. You may have held office as the secretary of a society (so you can put words together), or been a treasurer (so people trust you with their money), or perhaps a chairperson (budding management skills), or a volunteer (someone who puts other people first at least sometimes), or a minibus driver (someone who can be trusted with other people's safety), and so on. It's *your* story, so search your track record for suitable evidence of these other sides of you.
- **What makes you tick?** Some of the details about your hobbies or past employment may already paint a picture of this, but it's usually worth stating very carefully in your CV a little about your overall goals in life (at least your targets in the next year or two).
- **Who can confirm all this?** You'll almost always be asked for two or three referees, and be required to include their details when you complete application forms. More about these later, but it's worth including two or three in your CV too.

Get feedback on your draft CV

Ask as many people as you can to give your CV the once-over. The more people that you can get to read your CV, the better you can make it. Ask people to scribble suggested improvements and amendments all over it. You don't have to incorporate all of the suggested changes, but thank everyone profusely and then make good use of their best suggestions. Expose your CV to fellow students and learn from their experience. Show it to approachable lecturers and to contacts in business. Take note of any advice from people who themselves make professional judgements on the basis of other people's CVs. Sit back, now and then, and read your own CV as if you were someone else trying to decide whether they'd want to find out more about this person. Never regard your CV as finished. It needs to continue to change and develop as you do.

Should you have your CV done 'professionally'?

There are likely to be notices on boards in the students' union and elsewhere advertising people and agencies who will produce a good CV for you (and word-process your dissertation or thesis, and so on). What can these people do for you that you can't do for yourself? Quite a lot. They may be able to show you several styles and formats in which your CV can be presented, so you can choose which you feel will be most appropriate to you. Some are likely to have a lot of practice and experience behind them in putting together CVs. They may be able to offer sound advice about what to put in and what to leave out. They may be able to help you to make, in words on the printed page, the sort of impression you want to make. They may be able to make the final product look far more professional than you could.

So what's the catch? For a start, it will cost you. But the more important catch is that you could lose *control* of your CV. When you've got full control of your CV, you can tweak it for each individual application you use it for. You can update it immediately when you've got something new to add. It's also worth reminding yourself that any external agency or person can only produce your CV to the level of the information which *you* supply about yourself. You've still got to do the real work yourself.

A compromise can be useful. For example (if you can afford it), it can be worth trying out someone or some agency to do you a CV, so you can learn more about the whole process by getting involved in it. You can take due note of the things that turn out well in this experiment, and build them into your own way of building and *maintaining* your CV. Alternatively (again, if you can afford it), you may feel it worthwhile to enlist help in producing a CV for a particularly important application, especially if you've already got a really good version of your own as a starting point anyway, and perhaps at a time when you really have to get down to serious studying or finishing your dissertation, and so on.

At the end of the day, however, you'll feel more ownership of your CV if you own it! It's worth becoming able to produce a good document yourself. Employers prefer people who don't have to have other people to do their paperwork for them all the time. The word-processing skills, layout skills and editing skills that you can develop through building and maintaining your own CV can reap further dividends in your report writing, essay writing, dissertation writing, and so on.

▶ Application forms

The time you can spend dealing with application forms (and letters of application – see the next section) can be a serious hazard in the context of your final year. You still need to get that degree! But you need to consistently put your best foot forward in each application you make. However, there are several short cuts you can take to help you to handle job applications smoothly and efficiently. The more efficient you can make your job-hunting processes the more jobs you can apply for in a given time. The more jobs you apply for the better your chance of practising and developing your job-hunting technique, and the higher the probability that you'll land a really good first job.

Application forms and letters of application: what's the difference? In short, application forms are where you answer questions and provide information on the employer's agenda, whereas letters of application are under *your* control (in the same way as writing your CV).

What's so important about application forms?

There are several factors to bear in mind when you plan how you're going to organize filling in your application forms. The reasons why it's worth taking application forms seriously (but efficiently) include:

- **It's very easy for employers to *compare* application forms**. All the forms in the pile will look similar. At a glance, people deciding who to invite for interview can see:
  - which forms look the neatest;
  - which are the easiest to read;
  - who has the most relevant qualifications;
  - who seems to be the most interesting;
  - who seems to have taken the most care answering the questions.
- **Application form answers will be more relevant to the job than CVs**. The questions posed will often include ones directly relating to what is being sought for the particular post.

- **Application forms show employers how well you answer their questions**. This is obvious of course, when you think about it. It's no use just putting down what you *want* to tell them, if it isn't answering their questions.

Practise filling in the form

If you have to complete an application form using your own handwriting, it's important to work out exactly how much information, and what information, you're going to be able to write into each space on the form. If you try to squeeze too much information into a space, the end result is likely to look crowded and messy. If you end up putting too little information into a given space, it could look as though you have less going for you in that context than other applicants. It's difficult to edit your own handwriting without spoiling the appearance of the form. It's useful to make a copy of the blank form, and to draft out your written answers onto the spare copy, so that by the time you fill in the real form you have worked out exactly what you're going to include.

Fill in the real form in clear black ink, as it's likely to be photocopied at the other end. Not all colours photocopy well, and if your writing is too faint (or in some shades of blue), whoever does the photocopying may have to turn up the contrast on the machine to make your writing legible on the copies. This usually has the effect of making the copies blotchy, and gets your application off to a bad start in the overall appearance stakes.

Use your CV for information

Whether or not you send in a copy of your CV as well as the application form will depend on the instructions you receive. If you send one when instructed *not* to, your application will suffer; you could be regarded as someone who hasn't read the instructions properly, or who can't be bothered to fill in the form properly and expects their CV to make up for this! Whatever you do, *don't* send an unsolicited CV and write on your application form 'please see CV' instead of filling in the form! Furthermore, employers practising equal opportunity procedures may well relegate applications with unsolicited CVs to the bottom of the pile, and may not be willing to even accept the CVs. All this said, whether or not it is appropriate to send in a copy of your CV, it saves time to have your CV beside you while you fill in the form, as your CV should contain all the important information (dates, address details, qualifications, names and addresses of two or more of your referees, and so on).

Handwriting? What about typing the form?

Sometimes you'll be instructed to fill in the form in handwriting. This may be because the employer has access to a graphologist – someone who may interpret your handwriting to find out more about your character! Graphology is not (thank goodness!) an exact science, but it is claimed that some personality traits can be deduced from handwriting.

If you're *asked* for the form to be handwritten, you've got no choice but to get on with it. If there is no such instruction, and your handwriting is not too good, you may be tempted to type the form. That is, of course, if you can still get your hands on a typewriter, rather than a computer-based word processor. Typewriters are painful to use when you're used to word processing, as once typed, mistakes are hard to rectify and always show on the form, even if you use white ink or 'correcting' ribbons to disguise the mistyped letters. Also, if it's an old machine, with a fabric ribbon, the ink may have all but dried, resulting in typescript which is too faint to photocopy well. If the machine has a carbon film cartridge, the quality will be much better (provided the cartridge does not run out halfway through your form!).

If you're an expert with technology, you may feel able to scan-in the application form, and then use your word-processing skills (and your spell checker) to fill in each box as though you were using a typewriter. This may indeed impress the people who see the final result, but in practice it just takes far too long – you've got much more important things to do in your final year.

Another alternative is to produce your own version of the application form, by word-processing in the questions as well as your responses. The problem with this approach is that your application form will no longer look similar to everyone else's, and this could put you at a disadvantage. You can minimize this by making your own layout look very similar to the original form.

Yet another approach is to word-process your longer answers, print them, and cut them out and paste them neatly into the boxes on the form. This can look quite attractive with answers which are whole pages, or half pages, but gets very messy with your shorter answers, such as name and address details. A halfway approach, with short handwritten answers plus longer word-processed ones, gives an impression of inconsistency.

A further difference between typing and handwriting is that you can usually type a lot more into a given box than you could have written into it by hand. It's best that each box (at least those where you're expected to have something to say in response) is reasonably well-filled. A lot of white space might make your application look a bit sparse compared to others.

In the final analysis, the quickest route is usually to bite the bullet and simply get on and fill in the form by hand, having worked out carefully what you're going to say (and what you've got room for) in the first place.

Keep a copy yourself

If you're shortlisted, your application form is normally copied for each member of the interview panel you will meet, so you can safely assume that most of the information in front of them is what you put on your form. Interviews may be weeks or months after you've filled in the form, and you may have completed dozens of similar forms in that time. It's no use depending on your memory for the exact details you included on a particular application form – you need a copy. Before posting the form, either make a photocopy of it, or keep a draft version which has all the main details that you included on your real form. If called for interview, dig out your copy of the form and remind yourself of exactly what information the interviewers will have in front of them. This will be their agenda for at least some of the questions they will ask you, so it's important not to forget what they already know about you. Take your copy with you to the interview, and have a final look at it while you're waiting to be called in.

▶ Letters of application

It is quite common to be asked for a letter of application along with your application form (and perhaps your CV). Sometimes you may be asked to send *only* a letter of application, in which case it is obviously important to make it a good one. It is rare (but not unknown) for you to be *asked* to do your letter of application in your own handwriting. When there is *no* instruction to use handwriting, you have a chance to use your computer at last! It is also your chance to save time by making your own template on which to base all of your letters of application. With such a template you can edit up a one-page letter quite quickly, personalizing it to each particular job for which you apply.

What should be included?

Obviously, the letter should start with your name and address, and any other contact details, and the date of sending it. These can all be pre-programmed into your template. It is useful if the next information states clearly what this particular letter of application is about, for example:

Application by Sally Davies for the post of Technical Officer in the Department of Radiology, Western General Hospital

You *do* have to put the job title exactly as specified in the advertisement, as there may be several similar-sounding posts being appointed at the same time. You don't *have* to put the employer's full address and phone numbers – they should know who they are and where they are. However, it's quite useful to include their details so that *you* have them to hand for future reference, both on paper and in your computer.

Next comes your opening statement, along the lines of 'I am pleased to submit my application for the above post. Please find enclosed my application form ...' (and CV if included). It's useful to weave in the equivalent of 'as advertised in *The Guardian* on 27 February 2000'. This adds to the impression you may want to create that you're a well-organized individual and attentive to detail. They usually want to know, in any case, how you found out about the vacancy, as this helps them to keep track of which newspapers (or other ways of advertising) are bringing in the most promising applicants.

The next bit is the important one! In letters of application, your main job is to get them to *want* to find out more about you and to interview you. To do this, you need to cover two main issues:

- why you are particularly interested in, and attracted by, the prospect of the post, based on what you have already found out about it from the advertisement (and from any other source, such as a telephone call you may have made to find out more);
- why it is that *you* believe you are well-qualified for, and suited to, the post as advertised.

This means gently blowing your own trumpet for a paragraph (or at most, two). Weave in a little about any experience you already have that is directly relevant to the post. What you want to convey is 'I am an ideal person for this post, probably the best you're going to find anywhere', but in most cultures it would be quite unacceptable to put it like that!

Then you need to end your letter of application in a robust way. Something along the lines of 'I hope that I may have the opportunity to attend for interview, and to provide further evidence in support of my application for this post ...'.

Unless you're *only* sending a letter of application, it's best that you get the whole letter onto a single side of paper. It is easier for employers to look at single sheets, without the loss of continuity which occurs every time there's a page to turn.

Double-check your letter of application before you send it off, especially if you're adapting a standard template you've created. It's surprisingly easy for a sentence or phrase you composed for one particular application to get slipped into a completely different one. It can be useful to use a code for the main things you're going to fill in differently each time, such as the title of the post (perhaps xxx) and the date on your letter of application (or use an automatic date field – but print out a copy for yourself, don't just rely on keeping your copy on disk, or you may lose access to the actual date on the letter you sent).

As with application forms, it's vital to keep your own copies of your letters of application, and to be able to remind yourself about the exact words you used to put your case – you will be expected to justify your case and expand on it if asked for interview. Staple each letter of application to your copy of the completed application form. Staples are better than paper-clips – the latter have minds of their own!

▶ Choosing and using good referees

Let's start with the two most important things you need to do for your referees:

• keep them informed about what you're applying for;
• thank them for their help!

I've mentioned these things first, even before offering you suggestions about choosing your referees, because these are the areas most likely to get overlooked in your busy final year, and maintaining your referees' goodwill towards you is vitally important.

You will need referees for all of your job applications. They are the people who will be asked direct questions about your suitability for the posts you apply for, and also about your qualities as a human being. Most application forms have spaces for you to enter the names and contact details of two or three referees. It is usual to include two or three referees at the end of your CV, or on a separate sheet that you enclose with your CV. Even if you're simply applying for a post by letter of application, your letter will be expected to include the names of some referees.

What are referees for?

Employers need you to provide referees because:

• They need to be sure that applicants aren't just fabricating details about their qualifications and experience.
• However good your qualifications, they won't want to employ you if you're known to be unreliable, untrustworthy, difficult to get on with, and so on.

- Referees are usually asked to offer their own opinions regarding whether or not you are really suitable for the exact nature of the job you're applying for.
- The importance, or experience, of the people you choose as referees may be interpreted as an indirect measure of your own status.
- Referees are people that employers can ask for very specific information about you, if they wish – information which may not come through on application forms, CVs or your own correspondence relating to your application.
- If there are some unexplained gaps in your application, referees can be asked whether they know why this is so.

You need referees because:

- They can be really helpful in giving you their views about whether a particular application of yours seems to be a good idea to them.
- They may well alert you to posts you could apply for which you may not have been aware of from your own job-hunting activities.
- They will often know more about particular employers or organizations than you do, and can share this information with you, and alert you to things that you need to know.
- They quite often have their own contacts in firms or organizations, and if they're really enthusiastic about you and your application, they may sometimes make use of these contacts, informally, to back your case.
- They may prime you about the qualities that are being sought by particular employers or organizations, and help you to focus your application and interview.
- They may be willing to look over your applications before you submit them, and give you valuable feedback on your approach.
- They may give you further feedback on the design of your CV, and help you to develop it as you continue your job search.
- They may have a lot of experience in applying for jobs and handling interviews successfully.

All in all, well-chosen and favourably disposed referees can make all the difference to your job prospects. Conversely, if they are not favourably disposed towards you, they can sink your applications without trace, either by giving unfavourable references, or (more often) by what they *don't* say in their supportive comments about your application. If a referee *doesn't* mention that you're dependable, employers will interpret it that you're not! If they *don't* say you're trustworthy, the inference is that you're not! Therefore, maintaining your referees' goodwill is crucial. The two most important things you can do to maintain this goodwill were the basis for my opening suggestions in this section: keep them informed, and remember to thank them not just when you land the job you're looking for, but each and every time they work on your behalf.

Who can be your referees?

It is expected that at least one of your referees will know you quite well. More important, at least one should be in a good position to offer authoritative comment and opinion on your most recent work and life. This means that as a final-year student one referee needs to be an appropriate member of staff at your own university – someone who knows your work quite well (or very well), and who is in a position to report on it credibly. You need an established member of staff rather than a research student who happens to have become a friend. It looks better on your application details if this referee is patently well-qualified – a doctorate or professorship looks good. Alternatively, someone who is well-known in the discipline area (and well-respected, not infamous!) can be a convincing-looking referee. The best people to be your academic referees are likely to be busy academics – all the more reason for you to help them to do a good job for you by using their time wisely, keeping them informed about your applications, and maintaining their good disposition towards you by continuing to show your appreciation of their time and efforts on your behalf.

What about your other referees? You'll almost always be asked for more than one, and often be asked for more than two. It's normally best not to have both (or all) of your referees from the same stable. Employers are after rich sources of information about you, and if both of your referees are academics from your present university they're likely to have similar stories to tell about you. It is, therefore, useful for employers to check the consistency of their reports about your work, your qualities and your personality, but it is even better for them to be able to compare the views of people who have seen you in different lights in contrasting contexts.

Your second (or third) referee needs to be in a position to attest to your overall character, rather than just for the relatively immediate impression you have created about yourself at university. This means that it's useful for you to choose someone who has known you for some time, and seen different sides of your track record. Once more, it is helpful if your referee looks 'important' or authoritative on paper. Someone who is relatively distinguished helps. Normally, you're looking for someone who is an established professional of one kind or another. Doctors, solicitors, managers, researchers or teachers may come to mind. Of course, all that has been said earlier about having referees who are favourably disposed towards you continues to apply. Your non-academic referees may need more help in understanding the nature of the posts you apply for. You'll need to make sure that they are up to date about how you have grown and developed during your time at university – they may have known you better from your pre-university days.

What qualities should you seek in your referees?

This seems to be a contradiction – your referees are people who are supposed to be speaking about *your* qualities, so why should you be thinking about theirs? We've already seen that your referees need to be well-disposed towards you, and sympathetic to your applications, and to have a good understanding of the nature of the posts that you're likely to apply for. What other qualities should they have? Here are some further ones, along with short explanations about why they're important.

- **They need to be reliable.** You've got to be sure that if they're asked for a reference, at short notice, they'll get it in on time. Referees are usually asked for references with tight time deadlines, as most appointments tend to be made against the clock. If employers *don't* hear from one (or more) of your referees there will be plenty of other applicants where this problem doesn't apply, so your application is quite likely to be dropped from further consideration. On a more sinister note, when employers don't hear from a referee some assume the worst and take it that the referee doesn't want to say anything good about you!

- **They need to be experienced at giving references.** Like everything else, people get better at writing good references by providing them regularly for applicants. An experienced referee knows how best to represent your interests. A well-practised referee knows how to make you appear worth interviewing. A good referee can write between the lines! How can you find out how practised your intended referees are likely to be? You can ask them. In the case of your academic referee, you can ask other students who have used them. You can ask the departmental office staff – they may well know from typing out references for academics which are the best ones for you to go for.

- **They need to be people who will use their initiative.** For example, if time is short and they are not going to be able to get a reference in before the deadline, they can choose to fax it, or telephone instead of writing. Good referees will make sure that they get through to the right person in the firm or organization to speak to about you, and will check that the information they have given over the phone is logged.

Get your referees' contact details right!

This may seem like stating the obvious, but think about what can go wrong if you don't! Here are some of the things that happen every day.

- **A wrong telephone number is given**. The people trying to contact your referee can't get through. They haven't time to do all the things that *can* be done to track down the person they're after, and other people's referees are much easier to find. Your application sinks!

- **A wrong fax number is given**. References are often sought by fax, as by the time they are being taken up the interviews have usually been planned. If the fax goes through to a fax machine, people assume that it has been received by the correct person. My own home fax machine is one digit removed from that of a large company, and I get people's CVs and all sorts of confidential information sent to me – at least once a week. I now have an arrangement with the firm to send on (by post) wrongly-sent faxes, but when I'm not at home, that could be weeks later!
- **You get your referees' addresses, or titles or designations wrong**. This is more likely with academic referees than personal ones. Universities are large institutions, and there may be two or three people called 'Dr Jones' at your place. Postal mail often goes to the wrong person. If the person who receives it happens to be away at a conference or on a field trip, the urgent request for a reference could lie around for some time before being redirected to the right person. There may be even more people called 'Mr Jones'.

Any of these errors results in the same outcome – the reference isn't done. Employers who don't receive a reference are more than likely to assume the worst. It is therefore really important to make sure that your referees can be contacted easily. Make sure that you have as many details as possible correct. Try to get:

- university phone number or even better a direct-line number for your referee;
- departmental office number (where a message can be taken);
- the right fax number;
- email address, where available (double-check this by sending an email yourself, and making sure that you get a reply without any problems);
- the correct university postal address, including department or faculty or school, and postcode;
- your referee's home telephone number and address, if they're willing to share these with you (don't press too hard for these as some academics will regard receiving routine correspondence or calls at home as an invasion of their privacy).

Going to the extra work of making it easy for employers to contact your referees has the additional advantage that you are giving the impression of someone who is keen, well-organized and attentive to detail – all good indicators of the sort of person you want them to believe you to be.

I've already stressed that you should keep each of your referees up to date with the various applications that you continue to make, so that they are primed to reply when asked for a reference. It is also useful for you to keep up to date with *their* movements. For example, if one of your best referees is going to be out of the country for a month, you may need to indicate this somewhere in your applications, or choose another referee altogether for applications at that time.

▶ Handling lots of applications at the same time – keep files, not piles!

It's likely that you'll do many applications during your final year. Some of them will fall onto stony ground and you won't hear anything more about them, not even an acknowledgement of receipt. Sometimes you could be called to interview at short notice, in connection with an application that's been in the pipeline for quite some time. Whenever your applications are followed up, it is really useful to be able to lay your hands on *all* the paperwork to do with that post, straightaway, in one place, and without having to go through piles of past paperwork looking for the different bits.

If you can afford it, buy some cardboard wallets, and write the name of each job you apply for on the covers. Or get some old cardboard wallets, and use sticky labels (not Post-its!) to put the main details of the respective jobs on them. Make it a rule to have one wallet for one job. Put everything about the job into the folder, and add to it whenever there's more correspondence or further details. A well-planned job file could contain, by the time you go for interview, items such as the following:

- the original advertisement (with its source and date);
- a copy of your letter expressing interest and requesting further details, and/or any notes you made during or immediately after your telephone call to ask for more information;
- the further details sent to you, such as the person specification, details of the nature of the job, information about the firm or organization, and so on;
- your copy of your letter of application;
- your copy of your completed application form;
- your copy of the CV that accompanied your application;
- a reminder about which referees you gave and what you told them about the application, as well as anything they advised you about it;
- any notes you made to yourself about things you'd like to bring out at interview, or questions you'd like to ask.

It can be worth having a front sheet in each job file, on which you write key steps taken, along with *dates*. Having all of this key information on one sheet of paper at the front of each job file means that you don't have to plough through the whole file every time something new happens regarding that job. It's also a quick way of checking up on the progress of that application, and reminding yourself whether there's anything *you* might need to do, such as checking up, should you decide to do so, whether one or more of your referees have heard anything from the firm.

It saves you a lot of time if your job-hunting paperwork is in good order. Applying for jobs is only one of the many things you're doing concurrently in your final year, and you need to minimize the amount of time it takes. In practice, don't be surprised that most of the files turn out to be blind alleys. When you've not heard back about an application for a long time, or when you're informed by your referees that references haven't been taken up, you can regard those particular files as 'closed'. It is still worth hanging onto the files for a while yet however – your applications will sometimes be reconsidered, for example if the first shortlist turns out not to bring forward a successful candidate. Also, if an application of yours is unsuccessful, but the impression that it made was nevertheless a good one, you may be approached if a further vacancy arises in the firm or organization concerned. In cases like this it is really frustrating if you've already thrown out all of the information you once had – not least the exact wording of your original application.

When you've got lots of job files on the go, don't spend valuable time trying to keep your mind full of the various details involved in all of them. The trigger for you going back and having a closer look at any individual file will be one of two things: being called for interview, or hearing from a referee that a reference has been taken up. *Then* it's worth bringing the file concerned to the top of the pile and looking again at its contents.

To sum up, when you're called for interview it is much easier to be able to pull out *one* folder containing *all* the relevant information than to have to backtrack through a mound of papers pulling together everything relating to that particular application. You can take the whole folder with you to the interview, and refresh your memory of its contents, fine-tuning your mind to the context and details of the particular post in that particular firm or organization.

▶ Making the most of word processors

Most final-year students use word processors. You may well have learned to use one years ago, and have continued to develop your skills at word-processing as you did your essays, reports and coursework at university. Word processors bring two principal benefits:

- they help you to make documents look attractive, professional and authoritative;
- they save you time.

The first benefit is directly useful for your paperwork to do with job applications, but it's the time saving that can be the most important during your final year. Think of the various *repetitive* things you will write when you're doing lots of job applications. These include:

- requests for further details after you've seen job advertisements;
- letters of application;
- letters to your referees telling them about what you're applying for and continuing to thank them for their support;
- letters of confirmation that you will attend for interview as requested;
- your CV (fine-tuned for specific applications);
- your copies of any or all of the above, to keep in each separate job file.

All of these require repetitive writing. For each of them you can create a basic template which you edit and adapt for each successive application or communication. This means that you don't have to rewrite all the basic information each time (not least your own name, address, contact details, referees' details, and so on). It also means that you can gradually improve the appearance and structure of each of the letters or documents, and add second thoughts to their content and design as you see fit. Time saved in your final year can always be put to good use.

The fact that you've made yourself efficient at doing the paperwork connected with job applications means that:

- you can put in an application with the minimum of effort so that even when you're really busy with your studying you can find time to apply for jobs that come to your notice;
- you are far more likely to attend to the niceties, such as keeping your referees informed and thanking them, since it's so little extra effort to do so.

Using a word processor also means that you can save your job-related paperwork on disk. You can easily arrange job files on your computer, with a separate folder for each application. However, it is still important to have a paper-based file for each job containing everything, as your computer will only have *your* side of the paperwork for each job.

Don't be too colourful! A multi-coloured application looks different. With word processors and computers it's relatively easy for you to make your CV (and even a letter of application) more than just black and white. You *could* use colour for main headings or for running headers or footers, and so on. But towards the sharp end of the selection process it's almost certain that your paperwork will be photocopied, and this usually means it will be reduced to black and white anyway. Then colour can be a disadvantage, as some colours don't photocopy at all well.

▶ What happens at the other end?

All of the suggestions in this chapter are about aiming for your application to be buoyant enough to float upwards towards the top of the pile of applications received for each post you apply for. Sometimes there may be dozens, or hundreds, of applications.

Have you thought about how large numbers of applications are processed at the other end? The people taking the applications through the initial selection stages may not be the same people who will finally make the selection decision. It is common for administrators or junior personnel to do the donkey-work of looking through the big pile of applications, and reducing it to a much smaller pile. They will often do this on the basis of picking out candidates who seem to be appropriately qualified, by selecting those applications meeting some criteria they've been given regarding qualifications. They may even be asked to pick out applicants with a particular experience profile. It is likely to be these staff who carry out the routine correspondence relating to the applications, such as acknowledging receipt of them to candidates (where this is done – more and more applicants only hear back if they're being shortlisted).

Then, it's quite normal for the smaller pile (still often quite a large pile) of completed applications to be circulated one after another to a small team of staff, each of whom is asked to pick out the most promising half-dozen or so. Then, the applications which are most frequently seen to be promising are re-circulated to the same people and the top half-dozen (or more) of *these* are picked out and looked at more carefully. At this stage it's likely that references are sent for, relating to these applications.

Think about the effect of making a good impression during these early stages. A well-presented, easily-read application is always more likely to float to the top. Conversely, a poorly-presented, awkward-looking application tends to drift down out of sight, however good the applicant may have been.

As you can imagine, there's a good chance that things will get lost in the processes described above. Your application may go through several pairs of hands. If there are two or more separate 'bits' to your application (your letter of application, your completed application form, your CV, possibly a separate sheet listing the contact details of your referees, perhaps a continuation sheet where you supplied further details, and so on) it is all too possible that something important will get lost altogether, or become separated from the main body of your application. The chance of things going wrong is increased if any piece of paper in the pile *hasn't* got your name on it. If your name isn't unusual there is also the chance that there will be another candidate with the same name, and papers can get mixed up during the preliminary stages of selection.

There are ways that you can minimize the chances of things going wrong, each with its own pros and cons.

- **Staple your entire application together?** You should certainly do this with *your* copy of the application. If you staple the papers you send in, use one staple, near the top left-hand corner, making sure the staple goes nowhere near any of your writing or printing, and that all sheets are within the staple. Problems can, however, occur at the stage when copies of your original papers are made at their end. To make copies of the form itself, and perhaps your letter of application (and your CV if one was asked for), the staple will need to be removed. The parts of your application could then become dispersed, increasing the risk of loss. Moreover, staples can't be removed without tearing the paper slightly, and torn papers don't look so good when copied – the holes show!
- **Use paper-clips?** These avoid the problems due to tearing out staples. However, if you've ever handled large quantities of paperwork with paper-clips you'll know how often the clips seem to have a mind of their own and catch onto other papers from the collection. Alternatively, they seem to like to reside in the original envelope, or to escape to the floor as the papers are drawn from the envelope – in either case with the result that your application could become a set of loose papers from the start of the selection process.
- **Get it bound?** Some candidates go to the trouble of binding their applications using plastic spiral and punched paper, or using a document folder with a plastic spine to hold papers together. This makes for a good first impression, but becomes really troublesome when the main parts have to be photocopied.
- **Use a wallet?** This is perhaps the safest option. Gather all the bits and pieces making up your application in a plastic wallet, in the correct order. This also gives a good first impression. It is, however, even more important to make sure that every document bears your name and address, in case the plastic wallet is removed at any stage.

▶ Go for gold!

Apply for jobs! That should go without saying, but so many people don't get on and do it. I have often heard people say 'I really wish now that I'd gone for that job' or 'When you look at the person they actually appointed, I'd have been in with a really good chance!', and so on. Whenever you *don't* go for a job that might have been worthwhile you risk always regretting not having applied. If you don't apply you simply *won't* get that job. If you do apply the most you risk is not being offered the job, and a relatively small amount of wasted time and energy – not a lifetime's 'if only . . .'.

Personal action plan

Jot down two first impressions that you want readers of your CV to have about you, and add short notes about how you will generate these:

What's the worst thing you ever did when filling in an application form? How will you make sure that it doesn't happen again?

Make a short list of 'standard' details that you will include in your general template for a letter of application:

Jot down here the names of some people who could be on your team of referees. Remember to collect their *exact* contact details next time you have the chance:

Which of the above would you normally choose as your main academic referee, and why?

Which of your referees would you normally choose as a personal referee, and why?

Interviews and tests

▶ **Putting interviews into perspective**

When you're preparing for job interviews, they can seem a daunting prospect. Yet personnel selection interviews are only a tiny fraction of the interviews that go on all around us every day. To help you to feel less daunted at the prospect of being interviewed, here is a reminder about some of the other kinds of interview that are everyday occurrences. Another reason for alerting you to all these kinds of interview is that *you* are certain to be an *interviewer* in one or more of these situations later in your career. It's worth using your experiences of preparing for interviews now, and being interviewed, to help you develop your own toolkit of interviewing skills, as well as making sure you're as skilled as you can be at being interviewed yourself.

Types of interview

- **'Over the counter' interviews.** Almost every transaction in a shop or office requires some kind of face-to-face interview or negotiation, to establish and clarify data.
- **Advice interviews.** Whenever you seek advice (from tutors, student services, anywhere) you're involved in an interview situation. You are likely to be contributing directly to interviewing when you put your case or clarify what you're seeking, and you'll be interviewed when your adviser tries to find out more about your needs or wishes.
- **Travel interviews.** Arranging and purchasing tickets, planning routes, negotiating deals, whether at a travel agent's office or over the phone, involves you in practising many of the skills you'll need at interviews, whether as a candidate or an interviewer.
- **Phone helpline interviews.** Whenever you use these, for example to sort out computer problems, you're practising interview skills, such as

putting your needs across to someone else and developing the way you communicate using tone of voice, where body language can't help you.

- **Mass-media interviews.** You're likely to be a regular observer of other people's interviewing technique, and the ways that different people respond to being interviewed on radio and TV. These interviews can be among the most stressful for all concerned. Your turn may well come, as you become more famous!

- **Job selection interviews.** In the context of the other interview situations in this list, one significant factor in job interviews is that there is inequality between interviewer and interviewee, with the power weighted towards the interviewer.

- **Group interviews.** You may think first of being interviewed by a panel rather than an individual, but you may also be a member of a group that is being interviewed, such as a delegation taking their case to management or to a union.

- **Clinical interviews.** Another interview situation where there is inequality, for example between medical practitioner and patient, but which needs advanced interviewing skills to work well, as patients may not always be the easiest of interviewees.

- **Counselling interviews.** The interviewee is regarded as a client rather than a patient, and the lead in finding out what the client's needs really are may require highly developed interview skills on the part of the counsellor.

- **Police interviews.** Another situation with an unequal power relationship! The interviewing skills needed by police officers and lawyers are wide-ranging, not least because they are often in the position of trying to ascertain the truth from unwilling interviewees. This makes dealing with applicants for jobs seem like child's play.

- **'Cognitive' interviews.** These can be used to find out how successfully trainees are learning, or indeed how well *you* can give an account of yourself in a viva examination.

What's different about job interviews?

Compared to many of the types, and purposes, of interview listed above, job interviews are not particularly special. Interviewers in personnel selection are far less likely to be well trained in interviewing than (for example) counsellors, medical staff, radio and TV interviewers and people who interview members of the general public. Your job interviewers are likely to be quite naive, and quite unskilled compared to most other interviewers. One important and well-researched consequence of this is that it is claimed that most selection *decisions* are actually made during the first few minutes of most job interviews. You need to be aware of the likelihood of being stereotyped on early impressions. The good news about this is that it's well worth investing in systematic practice of your opening gambits for job interviews, especially your responses to questions along the lines of 'Now would you like to tell us about yourself?'.

Data-gathering, clarifying and probing

Interviews are question-and-answer affairs. There are three main types of questions: data-gathering, clarifying and probing. The data-gathering questions are the most straightforward. These are the questions you'll be asked about facts. In broad terms these include question words such as 'What?', 'When' and 'Where', and your answers to these are normally quite well-defined. Clarification questions ask you to throw a little more light on some of your answers.

Probing questions are the most important ones. These can ask you many things including 'Why?', 'How?' and 'So what?'. These are the questions that really sort out the candidates in job interviews. Interviewers may receive quite similar responses from different candidates to most of the 'What?', 'When?' and 'Where?' questions, but responses to the deeper 'Why?' and 'How?' questions will be much more individual in nature. It is with the probing questions that interviewers really sort out candidates. These are the questions not to rush into in your answers. Nor do you want to be too hesitant before you start to answer. Practising answering probing questions is the best way – and the only way – to develop the balance between thoughtfulness and confidence in your answers.

Getting safe practice at being interviewed

As with anything else, skill at being interviewed is best developed by practice. The more interviews you have, the better you become at responding to the unknown or the unanticipated. Get used to the sound of your own voice answering likely questions. Practise telling your story. Try out telling other people about your life, hopes, fears and ambitions – in two minutes or so.

One thing you'll have in common with most of your friends sharing your final year is interview preparations. You can be a great help to each other in this, and can save each other an enormous amount of time. Meeting up with friends from time to time and interviewing each other can provide you with realistic practice at handling interviews, in a really time-efficient way. You can script the main questions you expect to be asked, and pass them on to fellow students to fire at you. Encourage them to ask them in random order. Encourage them to ask them in different ways altogether, and to make up probing questions going behind your immediate answers. You'll learn even more by interviewing fellow students yourself. Playing interviewer tells you a lot about the impressions that people make when they respond to questions. Working out your own probing questions helps you to be better prepared for being probed!

▶ Maximizing your chances

Much of your preparation for any interview will already have been done, long before you set out for the interview itself. Writing your letter of application, filling in the application form, reading carefully the information you are given about the firm or organization, editing your CV to match the particular job, all are part of preparing your ground.

Don't lose all the ground you have already gained. When you find out that you've been shortlisted and called to interview, pull out the file or folder with all of this paperwork in it. Look through it all again straightaway, to remind yourself of the nature of the job you've been shortlisted for. Tune in again to the thoughts which you had while making that application. Remind yourself of why you decided to apply for the job in the first place. Don't worry if now that you look at it again you have second thoughts about the whole thing! You may well have applied for more interesting, or better paid, jobs meanwhile, but you may not have been shortlisted yet for these. An interview in the hand is worth several in the 'perhaps' tray.

On your way to the interview, look again through the words, your words, which will be in front of the members of the appointments panel. Re-read the information about the post. You may be surprised to notice, even at this late stage, things that you hadn't seen before.

When you arrive at the venue, keep your eyes and ears open. You'll often be able to gain useful information about the organization all the way to the interview waiting room. Don't miss any chances to talk informally to people you meet on the way, gathering information as you go. Be careful not to say anything which could be used against you in any way – you never know exactly who may be involved in some way with your interview, or whether the people you talk to could have some influence on those involved.

Putting your best foot forward

Success at being interviewed is strongly linked to your ability to put your best foot forward, especially at the beginning of the interview. I've already mentioned how important first impressions are, even before you say a word. What produces these first impressions? Some things are obvious, others less so. There is no second chance to make a good first impression! The following factors play a part in setting the tone for your interview.

- **Dress appropriately.** There's been all sorts of research on this! The short answers are that for young males, relatively conservative appearance is what is expected in most job interview situations. This means shirt, tie, jacket or suit, smart trousers, clean-looking footwear, and so on. You've probably played this game already at interviews – perhaps when first applying for university places, and certainly when trying for vacation jobs. You may well have applied similar dress principles when preparing for a viva examination, or other formal face-to-face situations at university. For female candidates, the research is less conclusive, and somewhat disturbing. It is suggested that for clerical or administrative posts, looking attractive and feminine is an advantage, but that for higher-level posts looking too attractive or feminine can work against candidates! A certain degree of formality is expected by some interviewers. Whichever your gender, don't underestimate how many assumptions, most of them quite unconscious, are made about your whole being when you walk into an interview room. Many of these assumptions may be quite wrong of course, and you may have plenty of opportunity to put your interviewers right about the assumptions they've made. But you won't always completely overcome some of the strongest assumptions, so the best thing to do is to make those assumptions favourable ones (even if incorrect ones!). In short, dress appropriately, and use your wits to decide what 'appropriate' means in the context of the interview. Plan your interview gear so that you have some leeway to 'dress up' or 'dress down' at the last minute – for example if or when you see how other candidates, your competitors, are approaching the situation.
- **Make a confident entry.** If you've acted on stage, or given any kind of public performance, you will probably remember how long it can seem between walking on and getting to where you're going to be when you start speaking, singing or playing. It may only take a few seconds, but these seconds seem to last for ever. You may be scared stiff of tripping up or falling over. Your heart rate may be twice its normal value! Your breathing may be tending towards fast and shallow – this you *can* control quite consciously. You may be sweating with anticipation, or even terror! The temptation is to rush. At interviews, this can be dangerous. Someone from inside the room will normally come to fetch you in. If you go in too fast, you may end up in the wrong place! There may be two empty chairs! Relax, and take your time to be shown to where they want you to be. Sit down when it is clear that that is what they expect you to do.

- **Smile!** Look your interviewers in the eye and make eye contact. Don't stare at them, but engage your gaze with theirs. If they look fierce, they'll normally at least smile back at you. When I say 'smile!', I don't mean go in with a fixed, maniacal grin of course! A nervous half-smile is fine. People react well to smiles when they are genuine and appropriate. Greetings are such an occasion. It does no harm to accompany your smile with 'Good morning' or 'Good afternoon' or 'Good evening' (but of course it does matter that you're seen to be in the same part of the day as everyone else!). This also gives you the chance to utter *your* first words, and hear the sound of your voice. You can also start to adjust the pitch of your voice. When people are nervous they tend to speak at a higher pitch, and faster than normal. Aim to start comfortably low, and sensibly slow.
- **'Tell us a little about yourself'.** Not all interviews start this way, but many do. It's really useful to have practised this bit. Your interviewers will often want you to say a little before they start asking their questions, not least to give you the chance to compose yourself and settle in. They may also want to compare the account you give of yourself with that given by other candidates. How much should you say? Too little leads to an awkward silence. But it's even worse for candidates to say too much, and to need to be interrupted so that the interview can get under way. Watch for body language cues which will indicate when your interviewers are ready to move on from hearing your account of yourself.

Answering *their* questions

This is of course the primary purpose of most job interviews. Your interviewers *may* have been well-trained, and will be asking all the candidates the same questions in the same order and in similar ways, and making notes (mental or written) of the principal points arising from candidates' answers so that they can compare candidates after the interviews. Alternatively, and more probably, your interviewers are not particularly well-trained at conducting interviews, and will be following their own whims and ideas to some extent as they pose their questions and listen to your responses. Whichever the case, you need to make the most of what *you* do. There are some ground-rules.

- **Silence isn't golden!** In general, silences during an interview are not good news. If you are stuck for an answer to one of your interviewers' questions, the ensuing silence feels like an eternity, and this undermines your confidence. If they are landed with an awkward silence, such as when one of your replies is too short, it leaves your interviewers with a negative feeling too. However, interviews are subject to time warps. What seems like an eternity to candidates is often a quite short and unnoticeable period of time to interviewers. There's a kind of a tightrope to walk regarding silence. If you try too hard to break every silence you will come across as nervous. It takes courage to pause quite deliberately, and think, and then answer in a calm and coherent manner.

- **Don't waffle!** When you're struggling to answer a particular question, it's best not to try to bluff your way out of the situation. When you're being interviewed by a panel, it's the person who asked a particular question who is likely to be making the most critical judgements about your answer. If you waffle, however, *all* members of the panel will realize that your answer is flawed. If you give a calm and confident answer, all the other members of the panel, apart perhaps from your questioner, may believe you've given a good answer when you have only given a moderate one! If you can continue this for everyone's questions, the net result could be that most people on the panel will think you've given good answers to most of the questions – that's your target in any case.

- **'I'm sorry but I just don't know!'** This is one way, and perhaps the only way, of handling those questions you simply can't answer. Admitting this from the outset is likely to impress all of the panel with your honesty, but also highlights to everyone (even panel members who had not really been listening until you said this) your failure to answer the question. You can, sometimes, lead away from your honest reply by continuing along the lines 'Instinctively, however, I think it is likely that . . .' and then giving your best guess. Or even admit it and say 'My best guess here is . . .' but try not to have more than two best guesses in the same interview!

- **Listen carefully to the question.** If you don't listen to a question you may end up not answering it at all. Sometimes questions can be quite long. Sometimes there will be more than one question wrapped up together. It can make a good impression to be seen to plan your response to complex questions. Imagine you're an interviewer and you've just asked a complex question, and the candidate replies 'I'd like, if I may, to answer your question in three stages. First, can I explain about so-and-so, and then may I state my position on such-and-such, and finally I'd like to offer my view about how to tackle the issue which is at the heart of your question'. If the candidate continues to go through these stages calmly and systematically, will you not be impressed?

- **If in doubt, seek clarification of the question.** Don't say 'I don't understand what you're asking' – this creates the wrong impression. Instead, offer *your* interpretation of the question back to the questioner, and check that this was what was intended. Most interviewers are only too ready to make sure that you've got their meaning correct.

- **Don't play politics too hard!** Listen to politicians being interviewed on radio and TV. Some are good at being interviewed, and many of the interviewers they're up against are far tougher than you're likely to meet at a job interview. And you haven't got the cameras on you, or the spotlights. However, politicians (and other public figures) are quite likely to have been trained to be interviewed effectively, and to handle hostile questions. Some of them develop the art of returning to what *they* want to say – even if the question asked of them is something entirely different – and getting away with it! This *is* an art, and not one you should try to perfect during your job interviews. If you divert each question towards something that you want to answer, your interviewers are very likely to see through it and interpret your actions as evasion tactics (which, in fact, they are).

- **Speak slowly, calmly and low.** Some of the credit for your answers at an interview goes with giving *good* answers, but some of the credit also goes with *seeming* to be in control of your answers. The less flustered you are the more confidence your interviewers will develop about your abilities. Actors and public speakers *learn* how to talk well, even when nervous. They develop conscious control of their breathing. You can do a lot of this for yourself during the practice I've advocated before interviews, and by using each real interview as a further occasion to practise.

- **Don't lose the ends of your sentences.** It is natural for voice pitch to fall towards the end of a sentence or an answer, but you need to make sure that your endings are easily heard. The ending of each answer is very important. It is also the trigger for the next stage – the next question.

- **Maintain eye contact.** When people *don't* look you in the eye when they talk to you, remind yourself how you feel about them. You probably don't quite trust them. You perhaps doubt their sincerity. If you find it hard to look people in the eye when you talk to them you need some practice at doing just this. You don't actually *have* to look people straight in the eye; you need to be *seeming* to do so. With a bit of practice you can appear to look straight at them, but not quite do so. You could be looking at a spot in space just in front of them, or just behind them, and they are unlikely to be able to tell the difference. Your eye contact is likely to be fine when you're really confident about what you're answering, so . . .

- **Make the most of the questions you're** *enjoying* **answering.** When you're finding it easy to give an answer you will come across confidently. When you're talking about something you're really interested in your natural enthusiasm will show – and enthusiasm is infectious.

It's good to enthuse your interviewers, not least about *you*. Besides, the longer you can talk confidently the less time there remains for anyone to ask you awkward questions where you may be less confident. At the end of the interview your interviewers will have a better impression of you if the lasting impression is of you talking confidently and interestingly. However . . .

- **Be ready to be interrupted.** Interviewers will want to move on to the rest of their agenda. It does not create a favourable impression if they can't get a word in edgeways because you're off on your hobbyhorse. Watch out for signs that someone is ready to come in with another question. If you're not quite ready for that, address your answers to other members of the panel who still look interested in what you're saying, but come back as soon as you reasonably can to looking at the would-be next questioner, and make room for the next question.

- **Don't be put off if your interviewers write things down.** It can feel strange if you're answering a question and people are making notes about what you say (your lecturers get used to this!). It can be tempting to stare fixedly at what they're writing, and to try to work out what it is, upside-down. However, this is not the time to worry about what they're writing. Some of it may be positive things about you or your answers. If it's not positive, you can't do anything about it at this stage anyway.

- **Respond to your interviewers' body language.** If you're interviewed by a panel, some will appear more agreeable than others! In other words, you're likely to get signals of encouragement from some members more than from others. Such signals include nodding, smiling, and so on. It's best to make the most of such encouragement at an interview, and to continue to talk particularly to the people who seem to be on your side. Don't, however, exclude other members of the panel. If you give them short change in your answers you won't have made friends of them, and the more friends you have at the time of reckoning after your interview the better your chances of being offered the job.

- **Be ready to make a good final impression.** There's no second chance to do this either. Last impressions can be lasting ones, and may colour interviewers' minds when they come to make their final decisions. When they've come to the end of *their* questions, it probably isn't the end of the interview, as they may ask you for *your* questions. I've given some hints on how to manage this stage of your interviews below, but for now, let's look at that business of ending an interview, for those cases where the end is *now*. It's important that your interview doesn't just fizzle out – that wouldn't be a good last impression. It can be an awkward moment, when there's not another question coming to you.

It can be another of those difficult silences, but this time it's *their* problem, not yours. Don't let it make you feel uncomfortable. Maintain eye contact with the chairperson or leader of the panel, continue to smile gently, and wait for directions. They'll either offer their concluding remarks ('We'll be in touch', 'Don't ring us, we'll ring you' or 'If you'd like to wait till we've interviewed the other candidates, we'll let you know' and so on). Or, more likely, it will be *your* turn to ask questions.

Asking *your* questions

'Have *you* any questions that you would like to put to us?' This comes towards the end of most interviews, and is a good signal that the event is almost over. It's an important question however, and you should respond to it. You can work out for yourself a list of questions *not* to ask at this stage. Don't, for example, ask earnestly about salary now, or paid holidays, or what time you'd be expected to turn up for work, and so on. This sort of detail you'll find out soon enough *after* you're offered the job. If you're not offered it, you don't need answers to these questions anyway!

This could be your best chance to make that good last impression. Think of two or three 'worthy' questions to have up your sleeve for this moment. Think through what you've been talking about during your interview. Think through what you've learned about *them* during the interview. What might they *like* you to ask? There are no 'right' questions for every occasion; you'll need to use your judgement. But, for example, there are plenty of safe options, such as asking a bit more about the firm or organization and plans for its overall development. You could ask about the kind of opportunities they might provide you with for further training and development. You could ask more about the general set-up of the post, for example about the nature of the team you might be joining if appointed. You could even be really bold, if the signs are favourable, and ask them what are the best things, in their opinion, about their own organization.

'Will you accept this job if we offer it to you?'

You won't hear this question at every interview. When it is asked, it is usually music to the ears of candidates. It often means that your interviewers have already decided you're a good candidate. It can mean you're the favoured candidate. So how should you reply?

If you say 'No', it means, one way or another, that everyone has been wasting their time at the interview you've just had. You might have really decided, by this stage, that you don't want the job, and there's no way of avoiding this uncomfortable moment. You could soften the blow a bit, and explain yourself along the lines of 'I'm terribly sorry, but now that I've found out so much more about the job and the firm, I don't actually feel that I'm very well-suited to the post, but I would like to thank you for your time in helping me to reach this conclusion, and for all that I've learned from talking to you'.

If you really, really want the job, the obvious answer is 'Yes'. But they may be asking this question to more than just you, so your 'Yes' needs to be a good one! In other words, your 'Yes' needs to be enthusiastic: 'I'd be really pleased to accept; when would you like me to start?' (But don't promise that you can start when you've already got other commitments you need to see through – employers *respect* people who see things through.)

'Yes' or 'No' are relatively straightforward; the difficulty is if the real answer is 'I don't know', or 'I don't yet know, I'll need to find out some more before I decide' or 'The answer might be "Yes" but I've got another interview next week, and I want to wait till I see what my choices are then' or 'Well, I might be persuaded, but what's going to be your best offer regarding my salary, working conditions, company car, secretarial help, and so on?'. Honesty pays, but not always! Any of these conditional replies can be taken as 'No' from their point of view – the next candidate who is asked the question may give an unconditional 'Yes'. So, there are cases when if you really don't know, the wisest answer could be a 'Yes', but perhaps a *slightly* conditional one. You could say, 'At this point I am *really* interested, but I have to say that I would need to get back to you within a week, by which time I will be in a position to give you a definite answer'. If they respect you for your honesty you may still be able to win the job. If they decide to offer the job to a more willing (or less scrupulous) candidate, that's their prerogative.

▶ **What about tests?**

As if you don't have enough tests in your final year! The fact is that many organizations don't just interview candidates, they test them too! The most common kinds of test are psychometric ones. These may be administered to candidates individually or in groups. They may be designed, conducted and interpreted by personnel consultants or firms brought in by large organizations to help sort out candidates into the 'right sort of potential employees' and the 'wrong' sort for their organization. Psychometric tests are carefully designed (it is claimed, by those who design them and sell their services to organizations) to probe into aspects of candidates' personality, attitudes, character traits and perhaps also into their interpersonal skills and transferable competences. If such tests were so marvellous they would be used by universities instead of, or alongside, final exams! This book is not the place to go into detail about the many kinds of test that are used. As with any other kind of 'test', the best way to become good at doing them is to do lots of them. However, your final year is not the best time to learn a whole new dimension of being tested and measured. The short answer is to read the test questions carefully, and think about what sort of answers to the various questions you think that they *want*, as well as deciding whether to answer the questions as you really feel!

Sometimes, you'll be given feedback on your performance in such tests. It's well worth finding out anything you can about the impressions or verdicts which were deduced from the analysis of your responses to the questions, and thinking back to which questions may have been responsible for any conclusions about yourself that you don't like.

Some organizations go to elaborate lengths to investigate the character and nature of personnel they're appointing to key posts. There may be a residential element of the selection procedure which is more akin to an outward bound programme than a job-selection process! Such extended selection procedures are primarily intended to measure how well candidates can demonstrate leadership skills, management skills, and team-playing abilities. You're not particularly likely to meet these time-consuming and sometimes quite gruelling selection procedures in the sort of interviews you get during your final year, but sooner or later you may have to prepare yourself to show your real potential under such circumstances.

▶ Keeping interviews (and tests) in perspective

If you've had a successful interview, and been offered the job, you don't need any advice about how to celebrate the event. Even if you turned the job down, you may rightly feel that you've done yourself justice, and feel good about the whole event. The time when you need to keep interviews in perspective is when you *don't* get offered the job. In particular, you may need consolation when you have been to *several* successive interviews and haven't come out as the winning candidate. I've listed below some home truths to think about under such circumstances.

- **Most interviews don't get you what you want.** Don't forget that business of making a shortlist. If you've made it to a shortlist you've already done better than most applicants for the job concerned. For many jobs, there may be half a dozen candidates interviewed, perhaps even more. This means that *most* good candidates don't get offered the job in the final analysis, for most of the time, at most interviews. There's no shame in *not* being offered a particular job on a specific occasion.

- **If they didn't offer the job to you it is quite possible that the successful candidate is more what they were looking for.** While this doesn't do anything for you, as a rejected candidate, it may not have been the job with *your* name on it. You may not have enjoyed it anyway. You may not have been able to do it well. You might have regretted taking it if you'd been offered it.
- **It has still been a useful learning experience.** Even an uncomfortable, difficult interview is a useful learning experience. Such interviews help you to develop your own technique, if only by trial and error. It might have felt like a 'trial full of errors', but it will still have helped you to improve your repertoire of interview techniques. It may make the interview which leads to your job offer that bit more successful.

The main thing to avoid is the slow-motion action replay of an unsuccessful interview. Don't give any time to thoughts of 'If only they'd . . .' – there's not much you can learn from what *they* did or didn't do at your interview. More importantly, don't agonize over the 'If only I'd . . .' agenda. Let it go. Tackle the if only agenda once only, and turn it straightaway into 'Next time, I'll try to . . .' resolutions for yourself. Write these down, then forget the circumstances that led to them. Build on the learning experience.

Feedback is always useful

When an application has turned out to be unsuccessful, you can still learn from it. In particular, it can be worthwhile to contact the firm or organization concerned, by phone or letter, and gently and politely request some feedback about why your particular application was unsuccessful. This usually works best by phone, where you can hear the tone of the replies to your questions. It is important that you don't come across as though you are challenging their decision not to appoint you. Occasionally, you may get some feedback that hurts, but resist all temptations to argue or defend yourself – you've more to gain by continuing to listen and receive feedback. Often there will be nothing that you could have done on that occasion to get the job. From time to time, however, you'll pick up something that you can put directly into practice in your next applications or interviews.

Personal action plan

What do you think is your best strength regarding interviews, and how do you plan to make the most of it?

What aspect of your interview technique do you most want to improve, and how will you get yourself some practice to help you to improve it?

How do you now plan to make use of the paperwork in your job file, when you find out that you've been shortlisted for interview?

What is the worst question they could ask you? Why is it a difficult one for you? Jot down three different ways of answering that question, then decide which is best:

What ideas have you at this moment in time about the nature of the questions which *you* will ask when you are being interviewed?

9 50 things to do in your final year

This final chapter is *your* agenda. It collects together a lot of my suggestions elsewhere in this book into a series of things for you to *do* as you work through your final year. You can't do them all at once, but if you were to do one per week you'd get through them all. However, that's not the best way to do them; it is better to work at several of them at a time, until you've got most of them under your control.

You could also use this chapter as a starting point to help you to work out for yourself what your priorities are going to be during your final year.

Don't take any particular notice of the order in which I've written this chapter – it just coincides, more or less, with the order in which I wrote this book as a whole. There's no 'right order' in which to tackle the checklist task. The best order is your own.

In choosing the things that make up the checklist I've tried to make each one:

- important (worth doing);
- realistic (not just good intentions);
- tangible (you can see when you're achieving it).

First, go through all the things in the list and give each your own priority ratings as follows:

 *** This is an urgent and important task for me, and I will give it high priority.

 ** This is quite urgent or important for me, and I will give it moderate priority.

 * It's worth me doing this, but it's not high priority.

 x I don't think this is worth me putting any energy into this year.

After you've sorted out your priorities, decide start and finish dates, particularly for the *** and ** tasks.

For some of the things, such as making decisions, you may be able to enter today's date when you begin, but there won't be a completion date. However, you could add a date that you plan to check that you're still following through the actions you decided upon.

As you work through your final year, and tackle all these things, take pleasure in entering in the final column the date when you finished (or more or less finished) each thing, especially when you've exceeded your own expectations and finished it early.

⊙ Task: final year checklist				
50 things to do in my final year	My priority ***, **, * or x	Date I aim to start this	Date I aim to complete this	Actual completion date
1 Check out my confidence levels: complete the task 'Assessing your confidence' in the Introduction to this book, and see which areas need most attention during the year.				
2 Do the 'diamond-9' exercise in the Introduction to work out what's really making me tick during this final year, and to establish what *my* ambitions and targets really are.				
3 Work out myself what are likely to be my main enemies during this final year: write them down, and jot down tactics that will help me to tackle them.				
4 Make the decision not just to *read* things, but to *use* them actively.				

50 things to do in my final year	My priority ***, **, * or x	Date I aim to start this	Date I aim to complete this	Actual completion date
5 Decide what classification of degree I'm realistically going to aim for (if this applies to my course).				
6 Write down the study avoidance tactics that I'm really very good at implementing, and ask a few friends what their best work avoidance strategies are.				
7 Make a list of five changes I'm going to make in my day-to-day studying habits, and post it on a wall where I can see it every day.				
8 Make three resolutions about improvements I'm going to make in my approach to time management, and post it where I can see it every day.				
9 Re-establish contact (phone or letter) with a good, old friend who's got nothing to do with my final year, and who may be able to help me keep it in perspective from time to time during the year.				
10 Check out my stress levels, and look carefully through the tips on managing stress in Chapter 1, picking out the three that are likely to be most useful for me.				

50 things to do in my final year	My priority ***, **, * or x	Date I aim to start this	Date I aim to complete this	Actual completion date
11 Read through the main things that are mentioned about 'learning pay-off' in this book, and make a list of my own of the learning pay-off I feel I'm getting from the main things I do regularly during my studying.				
12 Tidy up the way I refer to other people's work in my own writing, and set out to create a good impression by getting my references exactly right!				
13 For a piece of assessed coursework that I've completed, draft out three quite different attempts at an introductory paragraph, then think carefully about which one I'm going to use.				
14 For a piece of assessed coursework, draft out three ways of rounding off the piece in a strong, stimulating way, to gain 'last impression' marks, and ask a few other people which one they like best, before deciding how to end the piece.				
15 Reappraise the importance of *showing* what I know in assessed coursework situations, and write down for myself three ways in which I can become better at getting credit for what I really do know.				

50 things to do in my final year	My priority ***, **, * or x	Date I aim to start this	Date I aim to complete this	Actual completion date
16 Think about the lecturers and tutors that I know at present, and make a preliminary decision about which four of them may be most suitable (and favourable) to approach to be referees for me in the future (and think through how best I should help them to regard me more favourably).				
17 Work out what evidence I can produce to show to employers that I'm good at written communications skills, and start to build a collection of such evidence to be ready for my job-hunting stage.				
18 Learn to use (or improve my skills with) a word processing package, and decide what I'm going to use it on during my final year.				
19 Learn to use (of find out more about) email, and practise using it until I find it as natural as writing a letter.				
20 Review the planning technique that I use for preparing long forms of written work, such as essays or reports, and try out the essay planning approach described in this book.				

50 *things to do in my final year*	*My priority* ***, **, * *or* x	*Date I aim to start this*	*Date I aim to complete this*	*Actual completion date*
21 Think seriously about what is different in the level expected of me in final-year work, and make my own list of the ways I will try to demonstrate this deeper level in my work.				
22 Think about my writing style, and how best to research how well it is going to match the (perhaps different) expectations of the lecturers who will be marking my coursework and exams.				
23 Find out all I can about the assessment culture I'm matching myself to in my final year, such as by researching answers to the questions posed about assessment culture in Chapter 1.				
24 Make a list of 20 things I've got to show as evidence for what a wonderful prospect I am to potential employers, then set out to *find* and organize these pieces of evidence.				
25 Remind myself of the processes which I *know* don't have high learning pay-off when revising for exams.				
26 Set myself an early 'start date' for systematic, organized, non-hectic revision, and make that start.				

50 *things to do in my final year*	*My priority* ***, **, * *or x*	*Date I aim to start this*	*Date I aim to complete this*	*Actual completion date*
27 Map out a flexible revision timetable, including planned time off, plenty of variety, not sticking too long with any subject, and leaving time for those things that take longer than expected.				.
28 Consciously set out to find out something every day about 'what I didn't know I couldn't yet do', to pave the way towards becoming able to do it.				
29 Start systematically refreshing the things I've already learned, so that some of them get a few minutes 'polish' every day, and so that I don't get preoccupied with the things that remain that I can't yet understand.				
30 Think carefully through the implications of 'Working with a mate' (see Chapter 4), and decide how best to allow those closest to me to help me succeed in my final-year revision and exams (and keep the balance right so that I help them too if they're also studying for exams).				
31 Rate myself on my exam technique, using the exercise at the beginning of Chapter 5, and decide two potential improvements that warrant my attention.				

50 *things to do in my final year*	*My priority* ***, **, * or x	*Date I aim to start this*	*Date I aim to complete this*	*Actual completion date*
32 Plan out how to approach one of my exams, so that the time is shared out appropriately among the questions *and* a significant amount of time is saved for editing and polishing my answers.				
33 Spend a couple of hours, long before any of my exams, answering an old exam paper under exam conditions, then marking it myself, and seeing what I did best and what I could have improved.				
34 Research old exam papers, and other clues about what seems likely to come up, and start designing two or three exam questions every day, and practise thinking through what I'd need to do to answer them well.				
35 Find out about the alumni association at my university, and get ready to join it in due course.				
36 Talk to some people that are already doing postgraduate research, and ask them about the triumphs and disasters of being a research student.				
37 Think of some areas where I might be interested in doing research, and check out who in my university knows a lot about these areas, and talk to them.				

50 *things to do in my final year*	*My priority* ***, **, * *or x*	*Date I aim to start this*	*Date I aim to complete this*	*Actual completion date*
38 Work out what kind of research supervisor would ideally suit me, and make a list of the characteristics this person would need.				
39 Look at my CV as it stands, and find ways of making it serve me better. (Or write my first draft if I don't have a CV.)				
40 Look at three other people's CVs (one fellow student, one contact in commerce or industry, and someone else) and decide what's best about them and worst about them, and what I can learn from them that will be useful to translate into my own CV.				
41 Improve my CV and get feedback on it from one or two fellow students, one or two lecturers and one or two friends who aren't students.				
42 Choose one or two lecturers to be my academic referees, and approach them and ask them if they're willing to do so.				
43 Choose one or two people to be my personal referees, and have a talk (face to face or by phone) with them to check out how willing they are, and how suitable they may be.				

50 *things to do in my final year*	*My priority* ***, **, * *or x*	*Date I aim to start this*	*Date I aim to complete this*	*Actual completion date*
44 Pay a visit to the careers service and skim through the paperwork that's there. Make an appointment to go and talk to someone there about what I may want to become after getting my degree.				
45 Get myself a space to store the job files I'll be creating.				
46 Get some cardboard wallets to use as job files, and plan my system to make applying for jobs really efficient.				
47 Draft out a template for a letter of application, and print out one or two hypo-thetical letters, and look at how to make them *look* better and *read* more convincingly.				
48 Adjust my CV yet again, and ask for some more feedback on how to make it even better.				
49 Find some people (fellow students or otherwise) who are willing to play 'interview practice' role-plays with me, and get more used to hearing myself answer likely interview questions.				
50 Tape-record myself answering interview practice questions, and hear myself as I *really* sound, and decide whether there are one or two points about my manner that I can easily improve.				

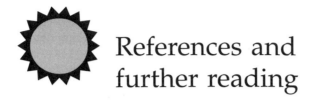

References and further reading

Bell, J. (1999) *Doing your Research Project*, 3rd edn. Buckingham: Open University Press.

This is a guide for first-time researchers in education and social science discipline areas. Its value is reflected in that it's been reprinted many times!

Blaxter, L., Hughes, C. and Tight, M. (1996) *How to Research*. Buckingham: Open University Press.

This book could help you decide whether the next part of your life will be as a research student. It could also help you with your final-year research project.

Blaxter, L., Hughes, C. and Tight, M. (1998) *The Academic Career Handbook*. Buckingham: Open University Press.

If after your final year your sights are set on an academic career, this book will help you decide whether you're making the right decision.

Brown, S. (1998) *The Times Higher*, 2 October, pp. 36–7.

Creme, P. and Lea, M.R. (1997) *Writing at University*. Buckingham: Open University Press.

Having reached your final year, you'll already be well-aware of the fact that a lot depends upon how well you write, whether in exams or in assessed coursework. This book could help you to check out that your technique is doing you justice.

Cryer, P. (1996) *The Research Student's Guide to Success*. Buckingham: Open University Press.

If your next career direction is going to be research, or even if you're already doing some in your final year, this book brings a wealth of experience to your aid to help you to keep on track, whatever your discipline area.

Delamont, S., Atkinson, P. and Parry, O. (1995) *Supervising the PhD*. Buckingham: Open University Press.

If you're going in for a PhD, you might like to buy your supervisor a copy of this. You can also use it to find out more about the sort of supervision that you need!

Denscombe, M. (1998) *The Good Research Guide for Small-Scale Social Research Projects*. Buckingham: Open University Press.

If you're heading for research in this particular area, you'll find an invaluable collection of advice here. The author leads you through how to do surveys, action research, ethnography, questionnaires, research interviews and the analysis of quantitative and qualitative data, and helps you forward into writing up your research.

Fairbairn, G.J. and Winch, C. (1996) *Reading, Writing and Reasoning: A Guide for Students*, 2nd edn. Buckingham: Open University Press.
This book is full of useful exercises and examples to help you improve your reading, writing and reasoning. The more effective and efficient you are at all three, particularly in your final year, the better your chance of succeeding.

McDowell, S. and Race, P. (1999) *500 Computing Tips for Trainers*. London: Kogan Page.
If one of your career options is to become a trainer, you might find this book useful. If you're wanting to make better use of email, computer conferencing, and the Internet, there are tips for you in this book.

Orna, L. (1995) *Managing Information for Research*. Buckingham: Open University Press.
If you're heading towards research, this will help you manage your time, transform your findings into appropriate written formats, and survive as a research student!

Phillips, E.M. and Pugh, D.S. (2000) *How to Get a PhD: A Handbook for Students and their Supervisors*, 3rd edn. Buckingham: Open University Press.
You'll know soon enough whether you're going to need this book. It's a 'goldmine of hints, sound advice, and carefully researched observations and lessons'!

Race, P. (1999) *How to Get a Good Degree*. Buckingham: Open University Press.
If you like my style in the present book, have a look at this one too. In this, my aim is to help students who are setting their sights high. Check out whether the suggestions and activities in this book can help you to get a better degree than you otherwise might have achieved – even in your final year it's not too late to improve your chances.

Yorke, M. (1999) *Leaving Early: Undergraduate Non-Completion in Higher Education*. London: Falmer Press.
An authoritative, erudite and readable analysis of what can go wrong in higher education. Don't spend your final year reading this, however, concentrate on keeping *out* of the non-completion statistics!

Index